UNIVERSITY EDUCATION.

BY

HENRY P. TAPPAN, D.D.

NEW YORK:
GEORGE P. PUTNAM, 155 BROADWAY.

M DCCC LI.

S. W. BENEDICT,
Stereotyper and Printer, 16 Spruce-St.

ADVERTISEMENT.

THIS Treatise includes an article published by the Author in the Biblical Repository of July, 1850. It was an afterthought to give it to the public with modifications and additions.

UNIVERSITY EDUCATION.

THE primitive idea and form of education is that of a preparation for the ordinary and necessary occasions of human life. The world was given to man as a vast store-house of materials, capable of being wrought out and adapted to his uses. As originally given in their rude condition, they met only his most necessary wants. But he had within himself the principle of a higher utility, leading to conceptions of convenience, comfort, elegance. The development of his nature in this direction gave birth to agriculture, the mechanical arts, manufactures, and commerce—the forms of human industry. This idea is the basis of what is strictly popular education. In its rudest state it presents merely, and in different degrees, mental invention, contrivance and adaptation, and physical skill—where instinct and spontaneous thought work together, and where the wonderful instrumentality of nature is perfected by use and ripened into habit. Thus we have unpolished men quick in calculation, and nice and skillful in mechanical works.

But human industry, in order to accomplish its most useful works, and to bring the physical conditions of the world to the highest perfection, calls in the aid of the loftiest sciences, both pure and physical: Mathematics, Mechanics, Astronomy, Chemistry, and the science of Nature, in its widest extent, are all brought in to aid and perfect human industry. The few here direct and govern the many. The people do not all become men of science, but they work by rules of a higher order which men of science have provided for them, instead of committing themselves to their own ingenuity, and to experiments more or less fortunate. But the employment of these scientific and determined rules quickens thought, excites curiosity, and leads to the knowledge of many scientific truths, and to some rational comprehension of the system of the universe, and of the power and scope of the human faculties.

Men, too, as members of the social organization, as subjects of government, as moral and religious beings, must acquire notions of social and civil law, of moral and religious duty. The cultivation of a people in this direction will depend upon the condition of their social state, the nature of the governments under which they are held, and the religious beliefs under which they have been nurtured.

We have in all the above particulars that form of education of which all men must more or less partake. It is the education of utility and necessary duty. It embraces what may be called a popular or practical system of education. Institutions which are established to promote this form are popular or practical institutions.

In nations, however, where the fine arts and literature are cultivated, the whole people feel the genial influences arising from the arts, in public buildings, in statuary and painting, and in the diffusion of poetry and music. And since, wherever the art of writing appears, a knowledge of written language becomes itself a matter of the highest utility in the ordinary commerce of life, there will be an effort to make this knowledge general. But this must bring along with it the possibilities and means of some degree of literary cultivation. Among the ancients, indeed, with whom books were scarce, the people in even the most cultivated states were dependent upon orations delivered in public assemblies, upon the recitations of poets, and upon dramatic exhibitions in the theatres, and not upon reading, for literary cultivation. But the effect of these was very great, as we see exemplified in the

Athenians. Among the moderns, the immense multiplication of books and periodical publications throws the influence of ideal and æsthetical education over even the lower orders. Popular education thus unavoidably advances beyond the mere demands of utility and necessity in industrial, social, civil, and religious life.

The second form of education relates to the arts of the beautiful, or whatever refines and embellishes human life through the influence of æsthetical tastes. The power of the arts is, indeed, felt by the whole people, but education in the arts properly belongs to a class. They are the men who are impelled by natural genius, co-operating with circumstances which often appear accidental, to devote themselves to an ideal life. Schools of art spring up with the spontaneity of the artistic life. Solitary endeavors—bright stars shining alone amid a wide-spread darkness—at first appear. Then the first great works form inspiring calls to kindred geniuses in after times, and stand as models of perfection and taste. Thus artists are multiplied. Next enthusiastic disciples collect around the great masters, and schools of art come into being.

The third form of education relates to professional life. The three great professions of Law, Medicine, and Theology, have their origin in the deepest necessities of man. They are *the professions* in distinction from all others as of paramount importance.

The first stands connected with ethics and civil jurisprudence—with the rights of man, the relations of individuals, communities, and nations—with social, civil, and moral order. Hence it demands a profound knowledge of moral science, of history, civil, political, and juridical.

The second is based upon multifarious observation and experiment, and involves a knowledge both of the physical and mental structure of man, and of the system of nature as containing both the causes and remedies of diseases.

The third, as developed in the Christian church, embraces a wide range of knowledge. The classical languages of Greece and Rome, together with their Hellenistic, Patristic, and Mediæval developments; the Hebrew and its cognates; History and Antiquities, sacred and profane; Metaphysics, Natural Theology and Ethics; and, since Christian doctrine has been mixed up with almost every form of philosophy, the fullest knowledge of philosophical opinion, and the history of dogmatic construction and modification, from age to age. These three professions collect as remedial powers around the cardinal interests of humanity. The first wars with wrong and injustice, and ministers to law, government, and the natural rights of man. The second wars with disease and death, and ministers to health, to the prolongation of life, and to both physical and rational enjoyment. The third wars with error and sin, and ministers to the moral perfection and the immortal hopes and well-being of man. And they all demand high gifts of intellect, and the noblest and profoundest accomplishments of learning. It is not surprising, therefore, that systems and institutions of education for the especial preparation of men for the learned professions should have grown up, and become paramount to all others; and that even the cardinal idea of a liberal education should have identified itself with the idea of such a preparation.

The fourth form of education is the ideal or philosophical. Here the capacities of the mind are considered, and the system of education is shaped simply for *educating*—leading forth—unfolding these capacities. We now leave out of view the mere utilities of life, the demands of particular arts, the preparations for a particular profession. We ask, what man is—what he is capable of becoming? We find him endowed with high powers of thought, observation and reasoning—with imagination and taste—with conscience and moral determination. And in all these he is capable of growing indefinitely—of becoming more and more intellectual, more and more beautiful in his imaginative and tasteful functions,—more wise and good, without an assignable limit. And then we ask, for the laws and means of promoting and leading on this growth? And we find that all knowledge is adapted to this great end,—that in knowing and reasoning he comes to know more easily and accurately, and to reason more rapidly and surely; that in forming an acquaintance with the great works of literature and art, and in producing these works, the imagination and taste are continually unfolding and ripening; and that the liberal professions and any employments entering into the life and well-being of society, while in their objective offices they are multiplying benefits on every side, react subjectively and form the discipline by which the soul grows into every form of intellectual power and moral worth, and becomes a partaker of the Divine nature.

Philosophical or ideal education does not abstract itself from the pursuits and ends of our human life, or lose sight of any of the great interests of the social state; on the contrary, it embraces them all, and that, too, under the highest points of view. It contemplates every man as having some proper work to perform for the common weal; but that, in order to perform it well, he requires the cultivation of all his faculties, while in the doing of his work, he shall ripen more and more. It has thus two states—the preparatory and the executive.

The preparatory is formal and scholastic, and comes under the direction of institutions of learning. Herein is cómprised that education of the mental faculties in general, of which we have spoken above. Man is a creature of reason, and therefore, his capacity of reasoning should be developed through all the forms and processes of logic in the prosecution of such studies as are judged best calculated to this end. He is a creature of language, and therefore should be taught the full power and beauty, and the ready and apt use of language in speech and writing by the study of the most cultivated languages, as presented in their classical works, whether of poetry, oratory, history, or philosophy, and by original efforts. He is a creature of imagination and beautiful tastes, and therefore should these be drawn forth in studies of the arts, and by poetry and music. He is a creature of passions and will, and therefore should be instructed in morality, and be disciplined to self-government. He is immortal, and therefore should he learn that system of religion which brings life and immortality to light.

Under the philosophical, or ideal point of view, Education is the cultivation, the improvement of man, in respect to the capacities wherewith he is constituted;

it is the nurture and development of his soul. Nor do we here forget his physical being, and neglect a training in all those manly exercises which give noble proportions, and hale vigor and strength. The ideal of a man is a true and cultivated soul dwelling in a sound and active body, prepared for all proper duties.

After a right worthy discipline of the man, by this preparatory course, we next proceed to the executive part of his education. Under this denomination we embrace professional studies such as Law, Medicine, and Theology, or th[illegible] relating to any course of life for which the individual may design himself. So much of these studies as are necessary to fit him for undertaking professional duty may also be pursued at literary institutions. But they require ever to be followed up and extended through life—as a workman would be ever handling his tools.

The education which we thus indicate by the philosophical or ideal is the most thorough, liberal, and extensive, and designed to make sound, disciplined, and amply-furnished men for the state and the church, and for all the arts, duties, and offices of life.

This conception of education is not that of merely teaching men a trade, an art, or a profession; but that of quickening and informing souls with truths and knowledges, and giving them the power of using all their faculties aright in whatever direction they choose to exert them. It seems, indeed, to belong only to the few who enjoy prolonged leisure for study, and a full supply of means and appliances to carry out this conception fully; but it contains a principle of universal application; for in even the lower grades of education, the true idea of education as the development of the soul in all its faculties, may be held up to view and acted upon. The reasoning powers will not be profoundly cultivated by the elementary branches of a common school, nevertheless they will be somewhat cultivated, and a taste may be acquired through them of the great end of study. Besides, let this higher notion of Education be adopted, and the human soul be treated not as a thing for secular uses, but as the lofty, lordly, and immortal subject for whose improvement and good all secular things are to be used, and then will the conception of its own value be infused, and it will aspire after its true cultivation, and those who direct popular education will aim to adapt studies to this end, unfolding it even under a limited education on those high and intellectual grounds, which its innate powers and best appropriation alike demand.

The conditions of human life may forever limit a thorough education to the few, but we see not why a valid principle of education should not govern every form and degree of it. With respect to those who design themselves for the learned professions, and for high and influential positions in the State, there can be no question that they require all the discipline of their best powers which they can possibly attain to, as well as that particular discipline and knowledge which relates to their peculiar calling. The first rears up men to their full stature: and the commanding places of society demand men of full stature.

Since some men are strongly determined by peculiarity of genius and taste to particular pursuits, and since the constitution of the world makes so loud a call for a division of labor, there will always be many who will press into professional studies without a thorough antecedent philosophical culture. Nor will we deny that eminent men in particular branches of science, and skillful men in art, and men of ability and efficiency in professional life, will thus be made. We will grant also that Educational Institutions ought to make provision for such cases.

But on the other hand, we ought to aim to make apparent the difference between a mere professional and technical education, and that large and generous culture which brings out the whole man, and which commits him to active life with the capacity of estimating from the highest points of view all the knowledges and agencies which enter into the well-being and progress of society. That is not really the most practical education which leads men soonest and most directly to practice, but that which fits them best for practice. It is not the mere use of implements of art which makes an artist, but the proper and artistic use of them. There are men who paint sign-boards all their days. In learning a trade, in gaining an art, in acquiring an education, there is some definite end in view, or there ought to be; time, means, and painstaking can be estimated only by this end. No one may arbitrarily say, there shall be so much time spent, so much labor performed, and then we shall have the trade, the art, the education; nay, but we must do all that is necessary to compass the end.

Now those Institutions of Education which are designed to stand pre-eminent, while they may give suitable scope to peculiar geniuses, and to those who set out to be eminently practical according to their own notions of a direct and ready method, must be so ordered as to lead, in the general, to a solid and thorough method. There never will be extraordinary wits enough to make a general law: and those who are bent upon the so-called practical method may do good service by their failures. But it is required of a great Institution of learning to make and vindicate a rule of education which takes its rise in the very constitution of man, and which calmly and majestically walking over the plausible but fleeting expedients of a day, meets with a sound heart and a strong hand the permanent exigencies of mankind

Men, ever prone to measure themselves and to measure each other, will also measure the character of institutions of learning by mere *success*. Now there is a great deal of success which is sheer good fortune, and much also that comes from keen-sighted but ignoble policy. Its emptiness is demonstrated by the fact that it sooner or later disappears and leaves no permanent good behind. Multitudes have no higher ambition than to gain a present success at whatever expense,—an element of human nature which has been set forth in that legend of a thousand forms—a blood-written compact with the Devil, by which the future is sold for the present. There are many who are so eager to grasp the bargain that they allow themselves to be cheated even in the present conditions of it, by becoming so intoxicated with ambitious projects at the first taste of prosperity, that they run against great principles which God has established in spite of the Devil, and thus are overturned in mid career. So frequently does this happen that a sage maxim has sprung up, that "honesty is the best policy." But this maxim, although it serves to restrain some, and to comfort others. is nevertheless left behind like a guide-board by the mad racers after success.

An Institution of learning may do a successful business in the way of multiplying empirics in Medicine, Law, and Theology; in furnishing men with just knowledge enough to make them political demagogues, or keen operators in all sorts of enterprises in this enterprising age. But there comes up before us in strong contrast with this, the idea of an Institution furnished with an ample and well-selected library, with a complete scientific apparatus, with well-filled cabinets,—with all the material of learning—an Institution with an enlightened and devoted corporation, with eminent professors, "many-sided" men, who, while intent upon their particular departments, are smit with the love of all knowledges and spiritual accomplishments, and so co-work together for the great purpose of building up human souls after a true and noble ideal, and preparing thoroughly-disciplined men to go forth into the world as ministers of truth and virtue, to adorn every profession, to labor in every sphere of duty, to sustain the state as majestic pillars, to carry forward every science with an earnest devotion, to add great works to a nation's literature, and to pour through every channel of society streams of influence to refresh, beautify and invigorate. Such an Institution will stand upon its own merits, and justify itself by its works. Its sublime position elevates it above the noisy region of mere success. It will do more for mankind if it should send forth only a few men of the right kind, than one that should pour forth a rabble multitude of sciolists.

In reviewing the history of literary Institutions, there are two facts which at once arrest our attention. The first is, that the highest schools of learning were chronologically first. Schools for the people were not the elements out of which Universities took their growth; on the contrary, Schools for the people grew out of the Universities. The second fact is, that Universities were not created originally by the State, but were the work of individuals. Solitary scholars commenced courses of public lectures which attracted pupils. Here was the beginning of the Universities. Afterward Colleges were endowed by benevolent patrons. The State gave its influence and authority only after eminence had been attained. "William of Champeaux opened a School of Logic at Paris, in 1109; and the University can only deduce the regular succession of its teachers from that time."* "The University created patrons, and was not created by them. And this may be said also of Oxford and Cambridge in their incorporate character,

* Hallam.

whatever the former may have owed, if in fact it owed anything, to the prophetic munificence of Alfred."*

"Colleges with endowments for poor scholars were founded at the beginning of the thirteenth century, or even before, at Paris and Boulogne, as they were afterward at Oxford and Cambridge, by munificent patrons of letters. It ought, however, to be remembered, that these foundations were not the cause, but the effect of that increasing thirst for knowledge, or semblance of knowledge, which had anticipated the encouragement of the great. In the twelfth century, the impetuosity with which men rushed to that source of what they deemed wisdom, the great University of Paris, did not depend upon academical privileges, or eleemosynary stipends, which came afterward, though these were undoubtedly very effectual in keeping it up."† It must be remembered, too, that this very enthusiasm for learning was created by the lecturers. So powerful was the fascination which Abelard exercised over his disciples, that the rude walls of the Paraclete in the solitude were no less thronged than the Schools of Paris.

In these two facts we have comprised the history of Educational development. Some solitary man gives himself to thought as the great end and interest of his being. He compasses the learning of his age, he ad-

* Hallam. † Ibid.

vances beyond it, he attains a deep consciousness of intellectual growth and power. The truths of which he feels himself possessed, the new system of philosophy or science which he believes he has unfolded, stir within him like an inspiration, and he is impelled to give fresh expositions of old truths, to correct current errors, and to proclaim his new doctrines. Other minds of similar tendencies, quickened into intellectual life by the fascination and power of his teaching, gather around him. He becomes the Doctor of a School. In some town or metropolis, or in some sacred retreat, he establishes himself. The number of his disciples increases, his fame spreads more and more, and he becomes a conspicuous object in the public eye. At length the noble and wealthy, ecclesiastics and princes, patronize the rising Institution, charters and privileges are granted, endowments are made, and it attains a permanent foundation.

Those who were disciples, now themselves become Doctors or Masters, and instead of the solitary man, there arise many lecturers in different departments of learning, and as rivals in the same departments.

In other places similar institutions arise, sometimes beginning with an exclusive devotion to a philosophy, or to the civil and canon law, or to a scholastic theology, and from thence in time branching out into all kinds of known learning.

The University now becomes the seat and fountain of knowledge. Here scholars resort. Here learned men are bred and take up their residence. Here from age to age the sciences are carried forward to greater ripeness. From hence go forth men to fill every profession, to hold great offices in the State, and to lead on the advancement of civilization and refinement.

The growth of a popular system of education out of the higher institutions is very evident. In the first place, it is plain that an unenlightened population will not themselves take measures for their own education. The very fact of a general ignorance, and a consequent want of taste and inclination for learning, precludes this. There must be certain enlightened individuals who are capable of appreciating and undertaking the great movement. The beginning of popular education must therefore, of necessity, lie in a higher region.

Now the communication of Universities with the masses of the people is twofold. First, they draw individuals from the bosom of the people within their cloisters, there to be nurtured as scholars. Secondly, they send forth among the people educated men in the different commanding offices of life. Every educated man among the people becomes the centre of a genial kindling influence, manifesting the power and diffusing the charm of intellectual cultivation. The stream of educated men constantly flowing out, leads to a constant influx of youths to be educated. Thus by two currents is the highest intelligence keeping up a communication with the lowest, multiplying the number of the learned, and narrowing the boundaries of ignorance, and making a sure and constant approximation to general education.

There were, indeed, formidable impediments in the way of the early consummation of this great and beneficent object. Among these may be mentioned the slow progress of the Universities themselves during inauspicious ages of superstition, tyranny, violence, and war; the extreme degradation of the people under the feudal system; and the appropriation of the Universities to the learned professions, and particularly to the education of the clergy. In some countries the Universities have never been emancipated from priestly dominion, and the influence of antiquated dogmas. Thus until lately the study of philosophy was prohibited in the Universities of Spain. Of course, where the Universities became the mere instruments of upholding systems opposed to human freedom and the general illumination of mankind, we can find no connection between them and popular education. But then let it be recollected that in these countries there is no popular education; while, on the other hand, it is just in those countries where the Universities have received the most extensive and thorough development, that schools for the people have been most multiplied and carried to the greatest perfection.

The history of our educational development must take for its starting-point the ancient schools of Greek philosophy. These schools were created by individuals who freely thought and freely taught. Disciples collected around them, received the light, and struck out new paths, and arrived at new truths for themselves. These schools existed without the patronage of the State. And it was a strange atrocity when the State, as in the case of Socrates, arrested the freedom of thought by persecution and death. Indeed, the schools rather patronized the State, for they gave that impulse to thought and disseminated those vital truths which, be they ever so abstract in the formal exposition, do, nevertheless, contain the springs of national greatness, for they make those great men the philosophers, the historians, the statesmen, the poets, the orators, the heroes who alone make a nation great.

The Grecian life was a life of thought, art, and heroism—and they co-worked together. Æschylus and Sophocles were soldiers. Alcibiades was a disciple of Socrates. Socrates was a sculptor, a soldier, a philosopher. Pericles was the orator and the hero. Pythagoras, the philosopher, the mathematician, the astronomer, by his political wisdom supplanted with his associates the ancient senate of Croton, and gave political constitutions to surrounding cities.

In these Schools of Philosophy, from Thales to Aristotle, was comprehended the metaphysics, the natural theology, the mathematics and astronomy, the logic, the physics, and the political wisdom of the ancient Greeks. They gave a manly discipline, they enlarged the boundaries of thought, they gave out truths which can never die. From these schools we have at least the imperishable philosophy of Plato, the imperishable geometry of Euclid, and the imperishable logic of Aristotle. We have also a form and method of education which has ever since been perpetuated, and lives to-day in our Universities.

The Romans only reproduced the philosophy of Greece. The school of Alexandria, the new school at Athens under the Romans, the Neo-Platonic—all the schools that came afterward had their prime fountains of thought, their methods and power, from the ancient schools. Oriental elements were indeed introduced, but the Grecian mind predominated. The schools of Law, of Medicine, and of Theology—all arose under the same con-

2

trolling doctrines and modes of thought. Galen even attempted to apply the demonstrative method of geometry to the science of medicine. Christianity came into conflict with the Schools of Philosophy, but she did not silence them. On the contrary, there was an interfusion of Platonism with Christian doctrine, and the logic of Aristotle moulded the forms of dogmatic theology.

The authority of the Church, however, prevailed. What she had received from the philosophical schools she baptized and called her own. The invasion of the Barbarians annihilated everything but the Church, and what the Church had taken into her repositories, or under her protection. The schools of learning established by the Emperors were converted into ecclesiastical societies, and all science and literature were merged into theology. The beginning of the eighth century showed the universal triumph of ecclesiastical power.

The theological education of Europe, from the fifth century to the beginning of the twelfth, was the mere study of the Fathers, and of commentaries upon them. Every doctrine was received upon authority. There was no free action of the human mind.

At the close of the eleventh century, Roscelin, the founder of the Schoolmen, appeared. Next followed William of Champeaux, the founder of the University of Paris. Now came the long reign of Scholasticism.

With the rise of Scholasticism is identified the rise, or the commencement of the modern development of European Universities. Scholasticism was really a struggle of the human mind for freedom and enlargement of thought against the authorities of the Church and the State. There could not be an open rebellion, there was not even the idea or the wish of an open rebellion. But the human mind, confined within the awful circle of ecclesiastical prescription, aimed, by Scholasticism, to make the most of its material, to find the best discipline of its faculties, and the widest range of thought. This was attempted by starting upon the received doctrines of theology, metaphysical questions, and deducing from them logical consequences. The Schoolmen were indeed nothing less than rationalists, who endeavored to present religious dogmas under the forms of the reason.

The great error of the Schoolmen lay in receiving both their religious dogmas and their philosophical systems upon authority. They studied neither the Scriptures, nor philosophy, independently. They relied upon the Fathers for their theology; and upon Plato and Aristotle for their philosophy. Their intellectual acumen appeared in attempting to reconcile the former with the latter. But it must be admitted in their justification that this error was forced upon them. The Church would not permit them to transcend authority by independent research. It was an age of authority. The Platonic and Peripatetic philosophies were curiously intermingled. The former had early influenced theological dogmatism, while yet the latter was excluded. The heretics were the first to introduce Aristotle. They made a skillful and powerful use of his dialectics. The Orthodox were therefore compelled to furnish themselves from the same armory. Thus in time Aristotle became the great authority, and the influence of Platonism apparently declined. Nevertheless, the Platonism already incorporated could not be discarded, but it was retained, and that, too, to a great extent, ignorantly, as the teaching of the Fathers. Aristotle was therefore the acknowledged authority of the Schoolmen, while in bringing him into union with the Fathers they were fusing the Platonic and Peripatetic systems together.

This will explain the celebrated controversy of the Realists and Nominalists. They were both wrong and both right. The former occupied the Platonic side of the question, and the latter the Aristotelian. Plato's ideas are realities—and must be acknowledged as such by every one who receives his philosophy—they are the seminal potencies of all knowledge in the human reason, and therefore as real as the reason itself. Aristotle's genera and species are but the names of classifications which may be natural, but are often arbitrary. They express only the common qualities which we take into view in conveniently arranging the particulars of the objective world. The Platonist, occupied with general terms as expressing ideas, the Aristotelian, occupied with the same as expressing a mere classification, are at issue only while they misunderstand each other's ground. It is plain that, contending under this misunderstanding, they could never arrive at a common decision. Hence the power of the Church and the State was called in to settle by decree, what no logical skill could terminate by the syllogism.

It was the prodigious interest created by these discussions, in an age when no other intellectual activity was possible, that drew together thousands of disciples around profound, acute, and eloquent lecturers. It was these discussions that brought the University of Paris into being, and gave new life to the old Universities, such as Oxford and Cambridge.

To estimate properly University education under the Schoolmen, we must conceive of theology as the grand subject of study, and the logic of Aristotle as the grand organon. There were, indeed, seven departments of study—seven being determined upon because the number seven was mystical and sacred. The first three, called the *Trivium*, were Grammar, Logic, and Rhetoric. These were elementary. The remaining four, called the *Quadrivium*, or the *Mathesis*, were Arithmetic, Geometry, Music, and Astrology. The last comprised both astronomy proper and the art of divination by the stars. These were studies of the highest order. But all alike were pursued in subserviency to Theology, and all were wrought into a vast speculative system determined by the forms of the syllogism.

Universities were thus an outgrowth of the Church, and destined for the service of the Church. They "seem usually to have grown out of cathedral or abbey schools, taught by the *Chancellor** of the Church; but his office became gradually external to it, and the teaching was carried on by persons who received his license; certain of whom were retained within the school itself, while by degrees, as these licenses became customary at the end of a certain course of study, a sort of external body grew up around the original school, yet within its precincts and under its protection. We have here the germs of many things. The *licenses* are the future *degrees*. The *esoteric* teachers foreshadow the University professors; and the exoteric lead us gradually to the lecturers in right of their degree, presiding over inns, halls, or hos-

* The Chancellor, *Cancellarius*, so named from the lattice-work behind which he sat, or from *cancelling* or crossing out writing, under the Roman Emperors, was a notary and scribe. In the cathedrals he originally was probably nothing more. In the Bishops' Court he is the Bishops' lawyer, versed in canon law.

tels—and thereby mediately or immediately to the tutorial system."*

The Colleges are not a part of the *University proper.* When students flocked to the lectures of the University professors, it was necessary to make provision for their lodging and board. For this purpose, inns, halls, and colleges were established. The inns and halls were [illegible], and finally gave way to colleges. These were endowed by benevolent individuals, and became permanent institutions. They were at first designed primarily for aliment and habitation; afterward, they were cloisters "for studious men to retire to, to devote themselves in leisure and freedom from the cares of daily subsistence, to meditation and the studies of the arts and sciences in general; always, however, as the handmaids of the *architectonic* science of theology, to which they were bound both professionally and academically."† The University, "original and essential, is founded, controlled, and privileged by public authority for the advantage of the State." The Colleges, "accessory and contingent, are created, regulated, and endowed by private munificence, for the interest of certain favored individuals."‡

* Quarterly Review, June, 1840.
† Ibid.
‡ Edinburgh Review, June, 1831.

"In the original Constitution of Oxford, as in that of all the older Universities of the Parisian model, the business of instruction was not confided to a special body of privileged professors. The University was governed, the University was taught, by the graduates at large. Professor, Master, Doctor, were originally synonymous. Every graduate had an equal right of teaching publicly, for a certain period, the subjects competent to his faculty, and to the rank of his degree; nay, every graduate incurred the obligation of teaching publicly, for a certain period, the subjects of his faculty, for such was the condition involved in the grant of the degree itself. The bachelor, or imperfect graduate, partly as an exercise toward the higher honor, and useful to himself, partly as a performance due for the degree obtained, and of advantage to others, was bound to read under a master or doctor in his faculty a course of lectures; and the master, doctor, or perfect graduate, was, in like manner, after his promotion, obliged immediately to commence (*incipere*), and to continue for a certain period publicly to teach (*regere*) some, at least, of the subjects pertaining to his faculty. As, however, it was only necessary for the University to enforce this obligation of public teaching, compulsory on all graduates during the term of their *necessary regency*, if there did not come forward a competent number of *voluntary* *regents* to execute his function; and as the schools belonging to the several faculties, and in which alone all public and ordinary instruction could be delivered, were frequently inadequate to accommodate the multitude of the inceptors; it came to pass that in these Universities the original period of necessary regency was once and again abbreviated, and even a dispensation from actual teaching during its continuance allowed. At the same time, as the University accomplished the end of its existence only through its regents, they alone were allowed to enjoy full privileges in its legislation and government."*

In time, salaried graduates or regents became permanent teachers; and these were peculiarly the *professors*. As the colleges multiplied, they rose in importance. They were placed under the care of masters, and finally lectures were delivered in the particular colleges in distinction from the University lectures.

The instruction given in the Colleges was at first a matter both of convenience and utility, and afforded individual students an opportunity of pursuing particular branches, whether from choice, or to make up deficiencies in those branches. With the exception of Germany, however, the Colleges finally obtained a prepon-

* Edinburgh Review, June, 1831.

derance over the University proper. On the Continent the Colleges did not become independent of the Universities. On the contrary, the regents of the Colleges were appointed from the University schools, and were always under the control of the faculties from which they were taken. "They formed, in fact, so many petty universities, in so many fragments of a university." Or rather, the University distributed itself into the Colleges. In England it was quite otherwise. Originally the government of the University had been exclusively committed to the masters and doctors in congregation and convocation; and the heads of colleges and college fellows shared in the academical government only as they were full graduates. Under the Chancellorship of Laud, the heads of the Colleges were clothed with supreme authority. In the Continental Universities, the University governed the Colleges; now, in Oxford, the Colleges governed the University. Hence it followed that the fellows of the Colleges became the tutors in their several houses by the consent of the heads of these houses. The professors of the Universities and the tutors of the Colleges now became rivals, and as the heads threw their influence on the side of the latter, the former declined. We cannot here enter upon the particulars of the process by which this great revolution was produced. But such was the fact.

The influence of this change seems to have been disastrous, and served to introduce into the English Universities an incompetent teaching. The Continental Colleges became petty Universities by receiving competent professors from the University itself. The English Colleges became petty elementary schools by exchanging learned professors for fellows, who were often made tutors by chance or by favor.

Leaving now the forms under which the University system was developed, let us return to the subjects of study. The reign of pure Scholasticism gradually yielded to branches more liberal—the ancient classics, mathematics, and physical science. The study of the ancient classics received a powerful impulse through the Italian schools, which produced many scholars of great eminence. The transition to the ancient classics was natural, from the common use of the Latin tongue. There was an affinity also between the logic of Aristotle and geometry. The study of the Peripatetic philosophy introduced the physics of Aristotle. The application of the Scholastic method to physical investigation made this branch of science indeed of little worth, and laid it justly open to the scornful denunciation of Bacon. Nevertheless there was progress, and the human mind was working up from the subtleties of the Scholastic philosophy to a region of greater freedom and light. The Universities were the centres of intellectual activity, where great men from time to time appeared, leading on the march of thought until the philosophy of Bacon changed the method of investigation, and Kepler and Newton revealed the true system of Nature.

It might have been expected, that with the advance of science, the Universities would have thrown off all the old scholasticism, and sprung forward in a new and glorious career. This, however, does not appear to have been the case so generally as the new era seemed to promise.

The changes in the French Universities were the effect of the convulsions of the Revolution, and the energy and patronage of Napoleon, rather than the result of a natural progress. The modern school of science and philosophy at Paris has been eminent; and the lectures of such men as Royer Collard, Cousin, Guizot, Jouffroy, Biot, and Arago, well nigh realize the ideal of a University.

In the English Universities the old tutorial and collegial system has continued to prevail. Oxford has been charged with the almost entire neglect of the mathematics, and Cambridge with a corresponding neglect of the classics. The Edinburgh Review of April, 1810, remarks: "We believe ourselves warranted to say, that the examinations at Oxford, till within a very few years, so far as they were scientific at all, and not confined to the learned languages, turned entirely on the Aristotelian and Scholastic logic. The college lectures, according to the best of our information, were guilty of this same neglect; they gave no account of the great modern discoveries, or of the method that had led to them. Some few individuals might pursue natural philosophy to a certain length; but it entered not at all into the general plan of education. To judge, so far as we have been able to learn, from the subjects of public examination, or from the general course of study, one would have thought that the fame of the great discoveries which had been made during the last hundred and fifty years, had never reached the University of Oxford."

Improvements have since been introduced, and greater improvements are in progress, particularly in the University of Cambridge; but it appears an indisputable fact, that the system of the English Universities has been lamentably deficient, and has by no means yet attained a completeness demanded alike by their long standing, and the character of the age to which they have come down. The Edinburgh Review of April, 1849, asks: "But, even as a preparatory training, is the actual benefit ever found to justify their high pretensions? Is there any man alive who can say, not with truth, but even with conviction, that the best or most laborious scholars and mathematicians of the University are the best lawyers, physicians, philosophers, or statesmen of England? The very reverse is the plain, if not the acknowledged fact. It would be difficult to find at present, among the most eminent leaders in Westminster Hall, any whose academical course was distinguished by studies, or crowned with honors, either mathematical or classical. The extent to which academical distinctions have lately been thrown into the background in the professional and public life of England, has gone lengths which really surprise us."

As a general system, the English Universities present us only courses of Collegial study of a very limited extent, pursued under tutors, and followed by examinations for a degree. The attainment of the degree appears to be the great end of study. Neither a principle of utility, nor of philosophical education, governs. There are indeed higher honors, the reward of higher studies. And unquestionably profound and elegant scholars are made on the foundations of the fellowships. We are speaking of the tendency of the system, and not of the opportunities afforded in these venerable seats of learning, to those who are disposed to study and learned retirement. But the men who should be permanent professors, like Whately and Arnold, can find at the Universities no amply-endowed professorships, or thronging classes yielding adequate fees ; and hence are compelled, with few exceptions, to take the head masterships of schools, or to retire into the church ; and leave the instruction to the fellows of the colleges. The truth is, that the English Universities still feel the incubus of the old Scholasticism, and reap the effects of the changes introduced under the Chancellorship of Laud. They are antiquated institutions, which do not meet the requirements of a new age.

As the Universities grew out of the Church, are in their origin Church institutions, their condition will be found to keep pace with that of the Church. Hence, in Spain, where the Schoolmen were longest cherished, and where the power of the Priesthood extended over everything, the Universities, instead of advancing with enlightened Europe, have remained fixed in scholastic and ecclesiastical solidity. In Italy they have retrograded.

On the other hand, in Protestant Germany, what an advance has been made ! In no part of the world has University education been so enlarged, and made so liberal and thorough. The Universities of Protestant Germany stand forth as model institutions, if there be such to be found; and the whole system of education, from the Common School upward, exhibits an intellectual progress which commands our admiration. In Germany, the emancipation of the Church was the emancipation of the Universities. The rationalism which now prevails, whatever may be its errors, is a symptom and a consequent of the intense reaction which there took place against the prescriptions of ecclesiastical and academical authority; and which must ultimately correct itself by the same force by which it came into being. The Universities of Scotland have exhibited a similar freedom and independence, without running into a similar excess. With a high tone of general scholarship, they have had also a distinct philosophical school of distinguished merit; and no country has contended more nobly and steadfastly for civil and religious freedom.

Now the English Universities exhibit the same correspondence to the church out of which they have sprung, and to which they belong. Two strong elements in the English Church have ever been, a zeal for the prerogative, and a stiff adherence to the apostolical succession. Many of us Protestants who have no great regard for either, think that the forced reformation of the English Church by Henry VIII., and the modifications which he gave it, never separated it sufficiently from Rome. It indeed received a new head, but retained many of the old errors. The Universities have in like manner been the strongholds of Toryism and high-churchism. The part which Oxford in particular has acted in our own times by her publications of a Romish tendency, and by the defection of some of her members, shows the direction and strength of her ecclesiastical bias. Oxford is governed by church influences, and these hold her in scholastic bondage, and bind her under a reverence for the past, instead of leading her onward with the awakening spirit of philosophy, and the enlargement of the sciences.

Neither Oxford nor Cambridge have ever had a school of philosophy. In this they have been left behind by France, Germany, and Scotland. England has had philosophers, but they gave no lectures, and formed no schools at the Universities. What had Bacon, Locke, and Coleridge to do with the Universities? What had the Universities to do with them? Ecclesiastical prescription can never allow a free philosophical movement. We can understand at this point of view the fact affirmed by the writer in the Edinburgh Review, that the examinations at Oxford, "so far as they were scientific at all, and not confined to the learned languages, turned entirely on the Aristotelian and Scholastic logic; and that the new logic, such as is explained in the Novum Organum of Bacon, was never mentioned." Professor

Whewell, of Cambridge, the learned author of the Philosophy of the Inductive Sciences, and of the History of the Inductive Sciences, has done much to awaken a philosophical spirit in that University, and has contributed essentially to the bringing about of manifest improvements in the course of education. His work On Liberal Education in general, is one of great value and interest. The distinction which he makes between *permanent* and *progressive* studies, is important and suggestive; the view which he takes of the discipline of the human faculties is philosophical and lofty; the proportions in which he distributes classical and mathematical studies, strike us as judicious; and his recommendation of the geometrical method in preference to the analytical as a discipline for the reasoning faculty, is wise and worthy of all attention.

That the English Universities are improvable, and improving, we fully believe. But never, while paralyzed by high-church influence, can they fully develop their great capacities, and collect within their precincts, and under their government, schools of philosophy and science formed of the great wits and profound thinkers of England. It is easy to get up scholasticism under prescription, but investigation and productive thought must be free as birds upon the wing—they must bear themselves along by their own native vigor, in their own native element. And we must run the risk of flying in the wrong direction sometimes, or we can have no flying at all, unless it be the wretched flying of a decoy-pigeon —fluttering within the limits of the string held by the hand of its master. Universities may, indeed, make learned men; but their best commendation is given when it can be said of them, that furnishing the material and appliances of learning, setting the examples in their professors and graduates, breathing the spirit of scholarship in all that pertains to them, they inspire men, by the self-creative force of study and thought, to make themselves both learned and wise, and thus ready to put their hand to every great and good work, whether of science, of religion, or of the state.

We have spoken of the German Universities as model institutions. Their excellence consists in two things: first, they are purely Universities, without any admixture of collegial tuition. Secondly, they are complete as Universities, providing libraries and all other material of learning, and having professors of eminence to lecture on theology, law, and medicine, the philosophical, mathematical, natural, philological, and political Sciences, on history and geography, on the history and principles of Art, in fine, upon every branch of human knowledge. The professors are so numerous that a proper division of labor takes place, and every subject is thoroughly discussed. At the University every student selects the courses he is to attend. He is thrown upon his own responsibility and diligence. He is left free to pursue his studies; but, if he wishes to become a clergyman, a physician, a lawyer, a statesman, a professor, or a teacher in any superior school, he must go through the most rigid examinations, both oral and written.

Collegial tuition in the German Universities does not exist, because wholly unnecessary, the student being fully prepared at the Gymnasium before he is permitted to enter the University. Without the Gymnasium, the University would be little worth. The course at the Gymnasium embraces a very thorough study of the Latin and Greek languages, a knowledge of the mathematics below the Differential and Integral Calculus, general history, and one or two modern languages besides the German, and Hebrew if the student design to study theology. The examinations are full and severe, the gradations of merit are accurately marked, and no one below the second grade is permitted to enter the University.

The Gymnasia thus guard the entrance of the Universities. Besides, the University course would not be available to him who had not prepared himself for it. It presumes certain attainments, and passes by the elements of the sciences. It is true, indeed, that a student may neglect his opportunities in the University, but then he throws away all hopes of professional life, and of employment in the State.

The Educational System of Germany, and particularly in Prussia, is certainly a very noble one. We cannot well be extravagant in its praise. Thorough in all its parts, consistent with itself, and vigorously sustained, it furnishes every department of life with educated men, and keeps up at the Universities themselves, in every branch of knowledge, a supply of erudite and elegant scholars and authors, for the benefit and glory of their country, and the good of mankind.

In comparing the University system of Germany with that of England, it is worthy of remark that Germany has also admirable common-school systems for popular education, while England is strikingly deficient in this respect. In the one case a properly-developed University system has reached its natural result of invigorating general education; in the other the priestly privilege of a cloistered learning is still maintained.

The Colleges of America are plainly copied from the Colleges of the English Universities. The course of studies, the President and Tutors, the number of years occupied by the course, are all copied from the English model. We have seen that in the English Institutions, the name of University alone remained, while the collegial or tutorial system absorbed all the educational functions. In America, while Colleges were professedly established, they soon assumed a mixed character. Professors were appointed, but they discharged only the duty of tutors in the higher grades of study; so that the tutors were really assistant professors, or the professors only tutors of the first rank. Our Colleges also have from the beginning conferred degrees in all the faculties, which in England belongs only to the University. By establishing the faculties of Theology, Law, and Medicine, some of our colleges have approached still more nearly to the forms and functions of a University. By assuming the title of University and College indifferently, as we are prone to do, we seem to intimate that we have some characteristics belonging to both, and that we deem it in our power to become Universities whenever we please. Sometimes the only advance made to the higher position, is by establishing a medical school; which, however, has little other connection with the college than its dependence upon it for conferring the degree of Doctor of Medicine.

If we understand aright the distinction between a College and a University, the latter is not necessarily constituted by collecting together schools under the different faculties. These may be merely collegial schools.

A University course presumes a preparatory tutorial course, by which the students have acquired elementary knowledge, and formed habits of study and investigation, to an extent sufficient to enable them to hear the lectures of professors with advantage, to consult libraries with facility and profit, and to carry on for themselves researches in the different departments of literature and science. A University course may be indefinitely extended at the pleasure of the student. He may here undertake the fullest philosophical education possible—passing from one branch of study to another, and selecting courses of lectures according to the state of his knowledge, and the intellectual discipline which he requires; or, having accomplished a satisfactory general education of his powers, he may next, either enter upon professional studies, or devote himself to some particular branch of science as the occupation of his life. In the German Universities any one, whether he designs to give himself wholly to a student's life, or to fit himself for a professor's chair, may, after undergoing the requisite examination, obtain from the faculty to which he belongs, permission to teach, without receiving any compensation, and only as a form of education. The professors extraordinary are selected from these licentiates, and receive a small salary. From these again the professors of the different faculties are usually selected. Every person of these three classes may lecture upon any subject he pleases: but professors are obliged, besides, to lecture on the branches particularly contemplated in their appointment. In this way at a University alone can the intellectual life be varied and enlarged. A University is literally a *Cyclopædia* where are collected books on every subject of human knowledge, cabinets and apparatus of every description that can aid learned investigation and philosophical experiment, and amply qualified professors and teachers to assist the student in his studies, by rules and directions gathered from long experience, and by lectures which treat of every subject with the freshness of thought not yet taking its final repose in authorship, and which often present discoveries and views in advance of what has yet been given to the world. In fine, a University is designed to give to him who would study every help that he needs or desires.

A College in distinction from a University is an elementary and a preparatory school. A College may be directly connected with the University, or it may not. Its original connection with the University was partly accidental, and partly necessary. It was necessary to provide convenient habitations for students who flocked to hear the lectures of the doctor or professor. Many of these students might require private tuition, in relation both to preparatory and additional studies, and thus the Colleges would become places of separate study, under masters appointed for that purpose. This must especially have been demanded in the early period of the Universities, when preparatory schools were not common.

In Germany the Gymnasia are really the Colleges. The education which they furnish is more thorough, we believe, than what is obtained at the Colleges of either England or of our own country. In England, schools like that of Rugby, under the late Dr. Arnold, and those of Eton and Westminster; and in America, those schools commonly called *Academies*, and indeed other classical schools, are of the nature of a college, only of a still lower grade, and more elementary. In passing from the classical school to the college the studies are not essentially changed, nor is the kind of discipline. Hence, a student in our country can prepare at the academy for the second, third, and even fourth year of collegial study. In college there may be less of juvenile discipline, and there are generally greater advantages. What gives the college, however, its chief distinction, is the power of conferring academical degrees. We may say, therefore, the academy prepares for the college, and the college prepares for a degree. In England the colleges are directly connected with the

University. But, it appears the University has fallen into desuetude, and colleges alone remain.

In our country we have no Universities. Whatever may be the names by which we choose to call our institutions of learning, still they are not Universities. They have neither the libraries and material of learning, generally, nor the number of professors and courses of lectures, nor the large and free organization which go to make up Universities. Nor does the connection of Divinity, Law, and Medical Schools with them give them this character. For law and medicine a thorough preparatory classical discipline is not required. In this respect the last is the most deficient of the two, and great numbers receive the academical degree of Doctor of Medicine who have never received an academical education. The degree of Doctor of Laws is more sparingly bestowed than any other; and this, as well as Doctor of Divinity, is never bestowed introductory to the entrance upon professional life. The schools of Theology approach more nearly to the University character than any other, since a collegial discipline is generally required preparatory to an entrance therein.

The course of study in our colleges, copying from the English, was, at their first institution, fixed at four years. The number of studies then was far more limited than at present, and the scholarship was consequently more thorough and exact. There was less attempted, but what was attempted was more perfectly mastered, and hence afforded a better intellectual discipline. With the vast extension of science, it came to pass that the course of study was vastly enlarged. Instead of erecting Universities, we have only pressed into our four years' course a greater number of studies. The effect has been disastrous. We have destroyed the charm of study by hurry and unnatural pressure, and we have rendered our scholarship vague and superficial. We have not fed thought by natural supplies of knowledge. We have not disciplined mind by guiding it to a calm and profound activity; but, we have stimulated acquisition to preternatural exertions, and have learned, as it were, from an encyclopædia the mere names of sciences, without gaining the sciences themselves.

"There are, in the whole four years, one hundred and sixty weeks of study. Suppose that the student pursues twenty of these branches of learning, this will allow eight weeks to each. Seven-eighths of the first year, and one-half of the second, are devoted to Latin, Greek, and Mathematics. If we subtract this amount, fifty-five weeks from one hundred and sixty, it leaves one hundred and five weeks to be devoted to the remainder. This will give us six weeks and a fraction to each of the other studies. But this is not all. In order to introduce so many sciences into the period of four years, the student is frequently obliged to carry on five or six at the same time; some occupying him three times, others twice, and others once in a week. In this manner, all continuity of thought is interrupted, and literary enthusiasm rendered almost impossible. Such has, to a greater or less degree, been the course pursued by all our colleges. The greater the number of studies prescribed in the curriculum, the more generous is believed to be the education imparted. When a college is not able to exhibit so extensive a course of instruction, it is considered as a misfortune which nothing can palliate, but its pecuniary inability to relieve it."*

At the same time that we have been enlarging this course of study, there has been a tendency to lessen the amount of preparation for admission into college, considered proportionally to the course to be pursued. We undertake to do more, with a worse preparation for doing it. But this is what might have been expected. A superficial system of study in the college will necessarily beget in the community a habit of superficial preparation. The highest institutions will set the tone of

* Report of Brown University, p. 15.

education. And this we see realized in schools of every grade and for both sexes. Our schools for boys, our schools for girls, present on the prospectus a formidable curriculum of studies, and immature beings of sixteen or seventeen are carried through the mathematics, the natural sciences, general history, the philosophy of history, belles-lettres, and metaphysics, together with two or three languages and various polite accomplishments. These higher branches, too, are often taught in lectures adapted rather to Universities than to elementary schools. The popular conception of education is not the orderly and gradual growth of mind according to its own innate laws fixed by God himself, but an immense and voracious deglutition of knowledges where the mental digestion is estimated according to the rapidity with which the subjects are disposed of. The more masters, the more books, the more branches of knowledge in a given time, the faster the process goes on. We educate as we make money, as we dig for gold, as we build ships and houses, as we make railroads and canals. Even in these the rapidity of our execution is not the sure sign of excellence and stability; but if it were, we forget that although we can quicken the labor of our hands, and increase the power and scope of our machinery, we may not overlay the organific power of nature; and that as trees must have their time to grow, and harvests their time to ripen, so the mind of man must grow from infancy to childhood, from childhood to youth, and from youth to manhood, and that as each period has its peculiar strength and capacities, so each requires its own nurture ; that many things may be accomplished at one stage of growth which are impossible at another; nay, that as the mind hath an immortal growth, there are some things that will be reserved for the discipline of eternity itself.

We have increased the number of our colleges to one hundred and twenty, that is, about four for every State. We have enlarged greatly the number of college studies. We have cheapened education—we have reduced it to cost—we have put it below cost—we have even given it away. The public has given money so liberally, and made education so nearly gratuitous, that, taking Harvard College as an illustration, every graduate costs the public nearly one thousand dollars. And, yet, it would appear from the Report of the Corporation of Brown University, we have lowered rather than elevated the character of our scholarship. "All of them (the colleges) teach Greek and Latin, but where are our classical scholars? All teach mathematics, but where are our mathematicians? We might ask the same questions concerning the other sciences taught among us. There has existed for the last twenty years a great demand for civil engineers. Has this demand been supplied from our colleges? We presume the single academy of West Point, graduating annually a smaller number than any of our colleges, has done more toward the construction of railroads than all our one hundred and twenty colleges united."—p. 18.

"The effect of this system on the mind of the teacher is equally obvious. He must teach, generally, from text-books composed by others. His mind can act but imperfectly on the mind of the pupil. The time of the recitation is commonly quite occupied in ascertaining whether the pupil has learned his daily task. He cannot mark out such a course as he would wish to teach, but must teach as much as he can in the fragment of time allotted to him. The books which he teaches soon become familiar to him. He has no motive to increase his knowledge, derived from the business to which he has consecrated his life. He already knows more than he has opportunity to communicate. There is no stimulus to call forth exertion. There is no opportunity for progress. The result is easily foreseen. Sometimes an instructor becomes interested in other pursuits, and his real business takes the place of only a secondary occupation. This is fatal to professional success. In other cases he becomes reconciled to, and finally in love with, his monotonous course; or, lastly, he throws up his calling altogether, and enters another line of life."—p. 19. From the same Report it appears, also, that notwithstanding the efforts made to enlarge the course of study and to cheapen education, the number of educated men has fallen off instead of increasing. The calculation is based upon statistics of the New England Colleges for the last twenty years.

It is argued, again, that so far from the intellectual character of the professions being elevated by the same causes, there is reason to believe that "the rank and file of every profession contains a smaller proportion of remarkable talent than in the last generation. The inducements to enter the professions seem to address themselves less successfully to young men of ability and enterprise. The other departments of life are continually alluring men from high places in Law, or even in Divinity. The productive professions are commonly filled with men who have not enjoyed the advantages of a collegiate education; nay, for whose benefit no schools whatever have been established, and yet, in influence, ability, and general intelligence, their position in relation to the professions is far in advance of that which they held some thirty years since."—p. 31. "The most coveted positions in society, seats in our highest legislative chambers, and even foreign embassies, await the successful merchant or manufacturer, no less than him who has devoted his life to what is called a learned profession. And yet more; the number of those who consider a collegiate education indispensable to a profession, has, for some time, been rapidly decreasing. Men have come to doubt whether the course which we pursue is that best adapted to prepare men for the duties of even professional life."—p. 21. The inference is, that men of distinguished talent avoid the colleges, and adopt some other mode of education.

The Report also shows, that notwithstanding the colleges have had in their organization an especial eye to the education of ministers of the gospel, and have been aided by Education Societies, the number of young men entering the sacred profession has by no means kept pace with the increase of our population. One fact is sufficient on this point. Six New England Theological Seminaries have together only eight more students now than they had twenty years ago.—p. 33.

But the condition of our colleges is represented to be such as to require relief not only to render the course of instruction more attractive and better calculated to meet the wants of the community, but also in many instances to save them from bankruptcy. The deficiency in the number of students, taken in connection with the low rates of tuition, renders their income inadequate to meet the current expenses, notwithstanding the endowments which they have received. This is shown to be the case of Brown University.—pp. 47, 48.

It is argued that if they be better adapted to the condition of our country, they will draw together a larger number of students; and that to make them better institutions, will be to increase their resources. —p. 50.

The particulars in which they are defective are,— First, The superficial education afforded by pressing too many studies within the four college years. Secondly, The requiring of studies which are calculated only for the learned professions, and particularly the ancient languages. Thirdly, The omission of those branches which are especially adapted to the mercantile, the manufacturing, and the agricultural classes.

The Report proposes to remove these defects by reorganizing the colleges on the following principles:

First, That the fixed term of four years be abolished, and that instead thereof courses of study be established in the different branches of learning, the time to be devoted to each course to be determined solely by the nature of the course itself. Secondly, That each student be allowed, within limits determined by statute, to select his studies for himself, and the number of courses he is to pursue at the same time, unless, in respect to these, the parent or guardian should place him under the direction of the Faculty. Every course, when entered upon, is to be completed without interruption; but any other course may afterward be added thereto, if the student so desire. Thirdly, Any student may take a degree upon sustaining an examination in such studies as may be ordained by the Corporation; but no student shall be required to take a degree. Every student shall be entitled to a certificate of the proficiency he may have made in every course that he has pursued.

The number of courses proposed is fifteen. These embrace the ancient languages, modern languages, pure mathematics, natural science generally, the science of law, the English language and rhetoric, moral and intellectual philosophy and political economy, history, the science of teaching, the principles of agriculture, and the application of chemistry and of science generally to the arts.

If the proposed changes should serve to increase the number of students, and thus both to sustain the colleges and to multiply the number of educated men, they would accomplish necessary and important ends. If they should farther break up the projects of distinct agricultural and mechanic schools, and collect the whole educational apparatus and all the candidates for education of the higher kind and degree in our colleges, they would effect an important concentration. Still more, if they should elevate the standard of education and give birth to more solid scholarship, they would claim our highest consideration.

An increase in the number of collegiate students, a concentration of the educational apparatus and of candidates for education at the colleges, might, however, be only a temporary success. New tastes and projects might arise and diminish again the number of students, and give rise to more popular institutions. But a change that should permanently elevate the standard of education, and give birth to solid scholarship, would be a benefit to be calculated by some other standard than the success expressed by the number of students. A few men of great and cultivated powers may do more for a nation than hosts of mere expert empirics, who without learning succeed in gaining a reputation for learning, and without principle, dare to invade the most sacred offices of society. The changes in Brown University may, through the effect of mere novelty, produce a rush of students to that institution at the beginning of the experiment. This, therefore, will not be accepted as a test of their value. But, on the other hand, when temporary popularity shall have passed away, should only the few great and commanding minds come forth and continue to come forth under these new auspices, then their character will be settled.

The question in education, as in religion, is not what men desire, but what they need. This must govern us in determining the form and quality of our educational institutions. Now when it is asked, What we need in the way of education? We may reply, either, that we need to fit men well for professional life, and for the general business of the world in the mechanical arts, in agriculture, and commerce; or, that we need to cultivate the human mind according to the philosophical or ideal conception; or, we might reply, that we need all in due order and proportion. The last reply would, unquestionably, be the correct one. We do need all in due order and proportion. Mere professional institutions will not meet our wants, for we do not all mean to be professional men. Mere agricultural, mechanical, and commercial schools will not meet our wants, for we do not all mean to act in these departments of life. Nor would we have the last without the former, for we generally mean to apply our education in the practical affairs of life.

It is a more serious and difficult question when we come to inquire after the due order and proportion. We believe that the due order and proportion exists only when the philosophical or ideal conception of education is made the architectonic conception, when the higher institutions represent it, and when, as an all-pervading light and warmth, it reaches to every grade of education. Human souls are to be educated because they are human souls: they are to be disciplined—to think, to reason, to exercise all the faculties wherewith they are endowed; they are to gain character and worth, to be fitted for duty, as human souls. This should be the leading thought of all education—of education in every degree, and for every purpose of life. When the lower ground is taken—that of making preparation for a particular art or profession, we shall fail of developing the full strength of the mind and of communicating the highest principles of action: when the higher ground is taken, we aim directly at the accomplishment of both. Nor do we in this way remove from education its practical character, since the development of the mind cannot be effected without setting before it its duties in general, and the particular offices in which society claims the services of human beings, and especially of educated men. We now, as before, enter upon the learned professions, or select some useful art or business, but we do it as men who know and who have cultivated their best capacities. However limited the discipline may be, it may still be conducted on right principles.

As to the defects in the system of education in our country, we have already given our assent to the Report of Brown University, in respect to the first; we believe that education has become superficial by attempting too much in the short period allotted. The other defects do not strike us so forcibly. A review of the college studies does not show an especial adaptation to the learned professions, unless it be in the space given to Latin and Greek. Indeed, the Report admits that it is not well adapted to the learned professions, and that good classical scholars under the received system are as rare as good mathematicians and civil engineers. Some of our colleges, too, have introduced a scientific course in distinction from a classical, to afford an opportunity to prepare for the other forms of life besides the learned professions. We think, too, that the idea of accomplishing a general discipline of the mind preparatory to any sphere of active duty, has not been absent from our collegiate systems. We confess, however, that this idea has not been well carried out and made effective. We have been aiming to do great things; we have called our colleges universities; we have tried to enlarge our course of studies more and more; we seem to have been struggling to afford every imaginable facility; and yet we have only a superficial and inadequate education.

Must we not seek for our great error somewhere else? We inspire no general desire for high education, and fail to collect students, because we promise and do not perform. Hence we fall into disrepute, and young men of ability contrive to prepare themselves for active life without our aid. In connection with this, the commercial spirit of our country, and the many avenues to wealth which are opened before enterprise, create a distaste for study deeply inimical to education. The manufacturer, the merchant, the gold-digger, will not pause in their career to gain intellectual accomplishments. While gaining knowledge, they are losing the opportunities to gain money. The political condition of our country, too, is such, that a high education and a high order of talent do not generally form the sure guarantees of success. The tact of the demagogue triumphs over the accomplishments of the scholar and the man of genius.

Put these causes together, and the phenomena we witness and lament are explained. Our colleges are complacently neglected when they neither afford the satisfaction and distinction of a thorough and lofty education, and yield no advantages in gaining wealth and political eminence.

We have multiplied colleges so as to place them at every one's door; we have multiplied the branches of study so as to give every one enough to do, and to satisfy the ambition of learning, if all are to be acquired; we have cheapened education so as to place it within the reach of every one; we have retained the short term of four years, so that no great portion of life need be spent in study; and we have made the terms of admission quite easy enough. Now all this would tend to the popularity of these institutions, if the education acquired helped us to gain money and political influence. But as it does not, it is not valued by a commercial people, and a people of political institutions like ours.

And even if our educational systems should be made more thorough, requiring more time, we see not that it would make a strong appeal to the commercial spirit and to political ambition, while men continue to succeed so well without high education. The idea of fitting our colleges to the temper of the multitude does not, therefore, promise great results. They do not answer to the commercial and political spirit of our country; nor to the philosophical or ideal—the architectonic conception of education. To attempt to make them answer to the former would be of doubtful success. But we can make them answer to the latter; and doing this, we shall meet every want of the human mind, and of society; for if we educate men as men, we prepare them for all the responsibilities and duties of men. And educating men on this principle, we should in due time have great examples of the true form; and the charm, and power, and dignity of learning would become apparent to all. And then education would stand out, as in truth it is, not as a mere preparation for the facile doing of the business of the world, but as the highest aim of the human being; as Milton has nobly said, "The end of learning is to repair the ruins of our first parents, by regaining to know God aright, and out of that knowledge to love him, to imitate him, to be like him, as we may the nearest by possessing our souls of true virtue, which being united to the heavenly grace of faith, makes up the highest perfection." In this way we should raise up a powerful counter influence against the excessive commercial spirit, and against the chicanery and selfishness of demagogueism which now prevail. Men thus worthily built up would get into all the relations of society, and throw a new aspect over the arts, commerce, and politics, and a high-minded patriotism and philanthropy would everywhere appear. Then it would be seen how much more mighty and plastic are great ideas and fundamental principles than all the arts, tact, and accomplishments of expediency. Then the host of penny-a-liners, stump orators, discoursers upon socialism, bigots, and partisans would give way before sound writers, true poets, lofty and truthful orators, and profound philosophers, theologians, and statesmen. We should have a pure national literature, and a proud national character.

To bring about this great change, we must do something besides multiplying colleges after the same model, pouring forth a tide of school-books, and making experiments upon a facile system of education full of pretension and fair promises, but containing no philosophical and manly discipline.

The multiplication of colleges after the same model only serves to increase our difficulties. We set about putting up the same kind of buildings; we create the same number of professors, to teach the same things on the same principle; we get together a few books and some philosophical apparatus; and then we have the same annual commencements, with orations and poems, and the conferring of degrees; and we get under the same pressure of debt, and make the same appeals to the public to help us out of it; and then with our cheap education, to induce many to get educated, we experience the same anxiety to gather in as many students as possible; and, since where we cannot get money it is something to get appearance, we show the same readiness to educate for nothing those who will submit to be educated, but who cannot pay. In all this we are improving nothing; but we are taking away all dignity from our system of education, and proving its inadequacy.

It were well to commence about this time some experiment of a different kind—a new experiment, and yet one of no doubtful issue, if we can carry it out to its issue. If we can give it a beginning and a middle, we know what its end must be. The establishment of Universities in our country will reform, and alone can reform our educational system. By the Universities we mean such as we have before described—*Cyclopædias* of education: where, in libraries, cabinets, apparatus, and professors, provision is made for studying every branch of knowledge in full, for carrying forward all scientific investigation; where study may be extended without limit, where the mind may be cultivated according to its wants, and where, in the lofty enthusiasm of growing knowledge and ripening scholarship, the bauble of an academical diploma is forgotten. When we have such institutions, those who would be scholars will have some place to resort to; and those who have already the gifts of scholarship will have some place where to exercise them. With such institutions in full operation, the public will begin to comprehend what scholarship means, and discern the difference between sciolists and men of learning. Then we shall hear no more inane discussions about the expediency of discarding Latin and Greek; for, classical scholars there will then be, who will have an opportunity of showing the value of the immortal languages, and the immortal writings of the most cultivated nations of antiquity. Then we shall have mathematicians prepared for astronomers and engineers. Then we shall have philosophers who can discourse without text-books. Then, too, we shall have no more acute distinctions drawn between scholastic and practical education; for, it will be seen that all true education is practical, and that practice without education is little worth; and then there will be dignity, grace, and a resistless charm about scholarship and the scholar.

The philosophic idea of education being thus developed in the highest form of an educational institution—where alone it can be adequately developed—it will begin to exert its power over all subordinate institutions. There will now be demanded a preparation suitable for undertaking the higher degrees of scholarship, and schools and colleges will receive a new impulse and will be determined to their proper form. We shall not now attempt to learn a little of everything in the lower institutions; but we shall learn that which is requisite to prepare for the higher, and we shall learn that well. The influence of the higher will be to give limitation, order, consistency, and thoroughness to the lower. And there will be diffused through all schools of every grade, and for both sexes, new ideas of intellectual discipline, and the sense of an elevated life and duty. Education now will have an authority to define it, examples to illustrate it, and the voice of a Divine spirit to call it forth.

We might have had Universities ere this, had we not wasted our means and energies in unfruitful schemes and misappropriations. We have wasted large sums in erecting expensive buildings in many different places for small collections of students, which, had they been concentrated, would have given for several uncertain colleges a stable University, with ample provision of books and the whole material of learning, and with endowed professorships.

Some of the States, like the State of New York, have made large appropriations from a literature fund to common schools, where, scattered in feeble streams through a thousand channels, it has produced no other effect than cheapening a little more what was cheap enough already. Massachusetts, with no literature fund, has a common and free school system no less, if not more complete and efficient, than New York. Common schools required no such attenuated patronage. But this fund, on an obvious principle of political economy, might have been concentrated into a power that would have given to the State of New York Colleges or Gymnasia, and Universities on an organized and connected system that would have justified her claim to be the Empire State, in a high and noble sense; and have made her, in her educational development, second to no country in the world.

The proposed changes in Brown University set forth in the Report of the Corporation, and which we understand have since been adopted, indicate that it is not preposterous to hope that some of our colleges may be brought under a higher organization. This Institution has hitherto been only a college, but it has been one of the best in our country in respect to its endowments, its library, and its faculty. It has also been one of the most respectable in point of the number of its students: nevertheless, it finds a change necessary, and it dares to make it.

There are some features of this new organization, which have very much the air of a University. The number of courses of instruction, the freedom of choice allowed to the student, and the abolition of the fixed term of four years, and the graduation of the time allotted to each particular course by the nature of the course itself—all these seem to point to a University. But the Corporation do not, after all, propose to do away the collegial character of their Institution, but only to modify it. Their leading conceptions are, first, the introduction of a better scholarship, by giving to each study more time, or not attempting to do more than can be well done; secondly, to adapt the Institution to the wants of all classes; thirdly, by this wider adaptation to call in a larger number of students.

The experiment alone can determine whether the modifications introduced will realize these conceptions of an improved and more widely-diffused education. We believe that an attempt to modify our collegiate institutions emanating from so respectable a source, cannot but have weight in determining other institutions to consider the necessity of introducing reforms into our educational system. We sincerely desire that the experiment may prove successful. And since the Corporation, in making the present changes, reserve the power of making still further changes, if called for, we shall entertain the hope that, in carrying forward this experiment, they may be led to form the purpose of making Brown University a University proper. As yet we do not discern the legitimate idea of a University.

The very conception of adapting the Institution to the wants of "young men who are devoting themselves to the productive professions," intimates that pupils will be received who have made very little scholastic preparation, and that, therefore, the courses intended for the "productive professions" will be quite elementary. The courses here proposed will undoubtedly be very useful to young men engaged in commerce and manufactures, and who propose to cultivate farms on scientific principles. The increase of students anticipated is likely to be chiefly from this class of youth; and thus, instead of the old college with its Greek and Latin, and Mathematics, shall we not have a large commercial institution, which, instead of gathering around itself classical associations, and impressing us with the worth and dignity of scholarship, shall only give us the hum of preparation for the business of life in the industrial and productive direction? The Latin and Greek scholars—the old-fashioned plodding students seeking after science and philosophy for their own sake, and dreaming of high mental cultivation and profound learning, will be rarely seen, we fear, when candidates for the "productive professions" form the overwhelming majority and create the *esprit du corps*.

We do not feel confident that this new organization will elevate the tone of scholarship. One of the principles laid down reads thus: "The various courses should be so arranged, that in so far as practicable, every student might study what he chose, all that he chose, and nothing but what he chose." This principle is intended to obtain universally, unless the parent or guardian should place his child or ward under the authoritative direction of the Faculty. Now it is possible for a student to choose either too much or too little, and either to renew the old evil of attempting so much as to lead to superficial acquisition, or to fall into the opposite evil of undertaking so little as to leave overmuch leisure on his hands. And we must not forget that these students are of no higher grade than those who usually enter college; youths, whose habits of application are yet to be formed, and their judgment ripened, and not, like the students of the German Universities, young men grown, and formed under the discipline of years spent in the Gymnasia, and who, therefore, may be presumed to have some ground to stand upon when they make choice of the kind and the number of the courses they are to pursue.

Nor do we feel confident that the colleges can be made the best institutions for all those who are devoting themselves to the "productive professions." Some who wish to become particularly scientific, would find such an institution congenial. But of the multitude who contemplate the productive professions, the majority will feel inclined to take a more limited course, and to enter as early as possible upon their apprenticeship. Indeed, we are doubtful of Agricultural and Commercial Colleges, however developed. We believe that the common schools, generally, can be so improved, or schools of a degree higher, branching directly out from them, can be established, where instruction in the principles of Agriculture embracing Chemistry, and in the application of Chemistry and of other sciences to the arts, can be more fitly and successfully given.

It appears to us that this plan of the Corporation of Brown University is defective, inasmuch as it attempts a union in one institution of three different grades of education, which can be more philosophically and successfully conducted in three different kinds of institutions. We have here combined something of the University, a good deal of the College, and a good deal of the Commercial, Manufactural, and Agricultural School, in which the one element may preponderate over the others, but in which a harmonious action of the three, and a suitable development of all, it is hard to conceive of. But, granting that this scheme should be followed by a reasonable measure of success; that, at least, it should sustain itself by the number of its students, still it cannot meett he highest educational want of our country, which, indeed, is the highest educational want of every country. It will not form the University where philosophical education can be carried out to its last results.

We feel no hostility to the experiment of Brown

University. The better it turns out, the better pleased we shall be. We shall even be happy to confess our error, if it shall appear that we have erred in any part of our criticism. The Report of the Corporation is an admirable one, and points out in a strong and lively manner the defects of our College system. The friends of the institution are now making a generous effort to place under its control the means of developing the new scheme. We cannot but feel a strong sympathy with this, and whatever may be the defects of the incipient movement, we repeat, that we shall cherish the hope, that eventually the noblest form of a literary institution may come out of it.

Another plan for improving our educational system is presented in the very able Report recently made to the Trustees of the University of Rochester, by the Committee appointed to draw up a Plan of Instruction for that Institution.

The University of Rochester does not profess to be a University in the strict use of the word: in reality it contemplates only a collegial course of instruction. The plan proposed and adopted aims to make this course more effective, by insisting upon an adequate and thorough preparation for admission; by adjusting the studies properly to the term of four years; by adopting two courses—a classical and a scientific—adapted to two different classes of students, the first to graduate as Bachelors of Arts, the second as Bachelors of Sciences; by limiting the voluntary plan to a choice between these two courses; and by demanding a mastery of the studies prescribed, to be decided by rigid examinations, ere candidates are admitted to the degrees for which they are enrolled. The Report expresses its leading principle in one sentence, "*Thorough* is the word which we need to have written upon all our seminaries and modes of teaching—upon the mind of every teacher, and on the daily task of every scholar."

The Report is filled with just and admirable views of education. In proposing an improvement of our collegial course, it undertakes a very important and necessary part of the great work of perfecting our educational system. If the University of Rochester is enabled to carry out its plan on the lofty principle it avows, it will make a real advance. We cannot but entertain cheering hopes of its success from the intelligence and liberal spirit which pervade the Report and from the names which are appended to it.

It is not necessary to our purpose to enter upon a critical examination of the plan itself. We only remark that the features to which we would take exceptions are those which are unavoidable under the present limitations of our educational system. We have only Colleges, and we feel the want of Universities; hence, we are continually struggling to give our Colleges as much of a University character as possible. "It would be a beautiful consummation to it (Modern History) if at an advanced period in the whole course, some higher instruction in History could be given by lectures, opening great philosophical views, tracing its currents in the channels of political organizations, viewing it in its connections with the science of Ethnology, and showing other aspects of this interesting subject."

We perceive here a looking forward to, a yearning after a University element. The whole plan bears marks, and we say unavoidably, of an endeavor to bring into the College as much of the University as the enlightened Committee deem consistent with their aim at a more thorough scholarship. The want exists and must be in some degree met, and until we have Universities in full, perhaps nothing better or more worthy of commendation could be offered. Still the limited term of study must preclude a ripe scholarship: and after the College course is completed with all its advantages, the student who wishes to pursue his studies still further will look in vain for an Institution to receive him. Indeed the Report itself announces the very feature of the proposed plan to which we have called attention. "The time devoted to what is considered a good education with us is entirely too limited to produce any high degree of scholarship. We deceive ourselves if we suppose that by any improvement in our systems we shall raise to a very elevated point the standard of attainments in any particular department of science or literature, unless there be evinced a disposition on the part of our young men to devote to their education a larger space of time than they are now willing to spare. When that period arrives, we shall be led to found great Universities, each one of which shall be the centre and crown of a system of Colleges, exerting a useful control over them and completing the education thus commenced. Until that desirable consummation, all that can be done is, to administer our Colleges wisely, and provide in them, as far as possible, the opportunity of more advanced instruction in some important branches, where it is now too limited to answer the ends in view." The College is thus proposed, under an improved form, to supply the more advanced instruction as far as possible until Universities shall arise.

While these commendable, although limited experiments are making in different quarters, all scholars and all true friends of learning will do well to inquire, whether there really be any good reason why we should not now create in our country at least one great institution of learning that may vie with the best of the old world. Have we not the means in abundance? Shall the little principalities of Germany surpass these wealthy and powerful States? Nor is it a question that such institutions are required to crown and perfect a system of education.

That the want of Universities is felt, is evident from the Report of Brown University, from the Report of the University of Rochester, and from the very evils complained of in the enlargement of the College course beyond the measure of the time allotted to collegial study. This general movement of the Colleges towards a higher position, by adding more studies to their curriculum, by endeavoring to shape themselves to more numerous classes of students, by introducing voluntary courses of study, by attempting lectures on the more advanced branches of study, and by assuming the name of University, is not a mere freak of ambitious folly, but an attempt to meet the demands of the age. The lofty-sounding curriculums of elementary schools for boys and girls, and the attempt to introduce University lectures even there, are indications also of an all-pervading idea which is striving in various ways to become realized. Now, everything appears crude and disjointed, and sometimes even grotesque: the fused elements are running in every direction, until they find the moulds which are to give them repose in proportion and symmetry.

Our Colleges grasp at a University amplitude of studies, at University capacities and functions, and take the name of Universities, and yet Universities they cannot be within the prescribed limits, with the general paucity of learned material and appliances, and while offering themselves as institutions for students in the elementary course. They were elementary schools of a higher grade in their inception, such they have ever continued to be, as such their existence will ever be demanded, and as such they require to be perfected. By retaining their original designation, while endeavoring to graft upon them what belongs properly to a University, we have only embarrassed them in their proper and possible functions, given them an equivocal character, and lessened their usefulness.

In order to perfect our Colleges, we need to bring them back to a more limited range of studies, comprising a thorough elementary discipline in languages and mathematics and other kindred studies, conducted with respect to a University course which is to follow. This University course might, in some of the older and more amply provided Colleges, be developed after the manner of the English Universities as they originally existed. The College, in this case, would not be enlarged to a

University after the present fashion, but the University would be constituted as distinct—beginning its courses of lectures just where the College completes its discipline of prescribed lessons and the recitation-rooms.

Between the University and the Colleges there would be no competition, and the relations would be altogether noble and generous: each would be necessary to the other, and tend to sustain the other; for without Colleges there can be no Universities, and in the Universities alone can the Colleges find their ripened results.

Education, in general, is of two kinds, and of two kinds only: an education imposed by tutors and governors; and an education self-imposed. The first relates to that period of our being embracing childhood and youth, when the faculties are yet immature, and knowledge is in its elementary stages. The second relates to that period commencing with early manhood, when the faculties are comparatively ripened, when elementary knowledge has been attained, and actual experience has taken the place of imagination and conjecture.

The first period requires of necessity authoritative direction, and plastic superintendence. The second period is competent, unless the first has been neglected and suffered to run to waste, to form plans, make decisions, exercise choice, and to apply itself, as from itself, to self-culture, the formation of character, and the duties of life.

All men do, in some sort, attain to both kinds of Education; for all men are disciplined in some degree, well or ill, by a controlling power in early life; and all men have some sense of independence and new responsibilities, when they reach the age of manhood. Education, of both kinds, is a law of our being more or less perfectly developed.

The idea of Educational Institutions, embraces the reduction of educational means and influences to method and system.

For the first period, various institutions have sprung up, from the most elementary Schools to Gymnasia or Colleges. For the second period there is only one institution—the University.

According to the present condition of our Educational System, the higher, self-determined, and manly course of study belonging to this period, appears only as an imperfect appendage to the College under the form of certain voluntary studies, and a limited range of lectures on the loftier sciences, conducted under manifest embarrassments arising from the want of a suitable preparation on the part of the student, and the inadequate amount of time covered by the Collegiate course. Hence, where the higher culture is gained, it is gained rather by studies pursued by the individual amid the duties and cares of life after the institutions of learning have been departed from, than by means of the institutions themselves. The culture which men, who are determined to make the most of life, attain to amid its active pursuits, is invaluable, and will be prized no less by those who have studied at the University than by those who have not. But who does not see the value, nay, the necessity of an Institution which opens its doors to us just when we escape from governors and tutors, and provides us with all the means, and affords us the example and fellowship of manly self-discipline? It is here alone that we can properly pursue the study of philosophy, which implies more than mere acquisition, and is the self-conscious growth of thought. It is here that we can become disciplined to independent scientific investigation, or lay broad and deep the foundations of professional and political life. It is here, also, that teachers and professors can be prepared for the scientific and classical departments of our educational institutions, in general.

The University thus stands just where the first period of education closes, and where the other begins. The second period, indeed, never closes. But as education, during the first period, requires for its orderly development institutions of learning; so education during the second, requires for its proper determination and successful prosecution, the formation of habits of independent thought and study, an acquaintance with method, and a general survey of the field of knowledge, such as can be gained only in an institution especially founded and furnished for these high ends. The University receives the *alumnus* of the *Alma Mater*, and ripens him into the man prepared for the offices of the Church and the State, and for the service of Science and Letters.

We do not entertain the doubt expressed in the Report of the Committee of the University of Rochester, as to a disposition on the part of our young men to devote to their education a larger space of time. The time which they now devote, is the time which has long been prescribed, and not the time which they have themselves appointed. On the other hand, the very pressure which the Colleges are under to enlarge their courses of study, shows plainly enough the demand for higher and more general education. We believe there are many young men who enter College smitten with the love of knowledge and with high hopes of a lofty education, and who now leave with disappointment, whose enthusiasm would at once rekindle at the prospect of a University. Nor is it an uncommon event for students now to seek in foreign countries for that which, as yet, they cannot find at home.

Besides, we must calculate upon the effects which would naturally follow the creation of Universities. They would stand before the community as the culmination of our educational system,—as containing everything to meet the highest wants and aspirations of the human mind,—as spreading out the fair fields of knowledge to their utmost extent,—as presenting an invitation to the ripest cultivation of every branch of science and literature,—as opening retreats where the studious may retire in the fullest satisfaction,—as affording the highest possibilities, and stimulating the noblest endeavors. There would now no longer exist any temptation or necessity for the Colleges to make more or less successful, more or less abortive attempts to pass beyond their just measure, and to sacrifice their invaluable offices and benefits in trespassing upon grounds which do not naturally belong to them. They would explode those jejune schemes of education which seek to introduce juvenile minds, in the incipient stages of discipline, to the higher forms of education for which they have acquired no preparation. They would define clearly the distinction between an elementary and preparatory discipline, and that independent and manly and self-determined pursuit of knowledge which belongs to students who have learned the art of study, and who know how to avail themselves of books and the lectures of distinguished and finished scholars. Hence they would introduce order, method, and consistency into the whole course of education. Now, in entering upon the very first stages of education, the student would have the whole line of progress clearly marked out before him; he would know the point to which he is tending, and where he might, without uncertainty, realize his highest hopes. The spirit of scholarship would thus be thoroughly awakened, the life of a scholar be clearly defined, and, instead of calculating the time of study, his regards would be fixed upon the ends of study—the glorious attainments to be realized.

William of Champeaux did not wait until the spirit of scholarship had permeated masses of men: he commenced his lectures, laid the foundations of a University, and created the spirit of scholarship. In our country and age, we are not called upon to create the spirit of scholarship, it already exists; we have only to inform it with ideas, and to quicken it to a higher life.

We hold, therefore, that Universities are natural and necessary institutions in a great system of public education. To delay their creation is to stop the hand upon the dial-plate which represents the progress of humanity.

We have delayed this great work of founding Universities too long. We cannot well afford to wait for any new sign from heaven before we begin this work. Is there any impertinence in calling upon all scholars and true friends of learning to consider whether we may not now create at least one great institution of learning that may vie with the best of the old world? And if we designed to show the spirit of this undertaking in a few words, we would say, that it is required for the successful development of such an institution, that it should neither cheapen its education at the expense of its intellectual life and aliment, nor be tempted to do so; that it should be adequate to educate the many, and yet not be destroyed if compelled, for a time, to educate the few; that it should be removed alike from the conflicts and jealousies of sects in the Church, and of parties in the State; and that it should be faithfully consecrated to science, literature, and art.

No part of our country presents equal facilities with the city of New York, for carrying out this great undertaking. New York is really the metropolitan city of our country. The centre of commercial activity, the vast reservoir of wealth, it takes the lead in the elegancies and splendor of life, in the arts of luxury and amusement. It is also the great emporium of books and the fine arts. Here resort the professors of music and of the arts of design. Here literary men are taking up their abode. Here literary institutions of various kinds and grades have already come into being. Here are libraries established by associations or by individual munificence, which are enlarging themselves from year to year. Commerce, wealth, and elegance invite, nay, demand the invigorating life, the counterbalancing power and activity of intellectual cultivation. Whatever is requisite for a great Institution of Learning can here be most readily collected; and here are the means in profusion of creating whatever the well-being and glory of our city and of our country may require. By adding to the natural attractions of a metropolitan city the attractions of literature, science, and art, as embodied in a great University, students from every part of the Union would be naturally drawn together. We should thus have a fully appointed national Institution where the bonds of our nationality would be strengthened by the loftiest form of education, the sympathy of scholars, and the noblest productions of literature.

A great Institution would collect together all that is now scattered and isolated among us, be the home of scholars, the nurse of scholarlike endeavors, the regulating and harmonizing centre of thought and investigation. Our whole population would feel the plastic power of intellectual development and progress; society would receive new forms and habitudes from a learned class, and knowledges be widely diffused by public lectures under the direction of an elite corporation.

But what shall be the form of this Institution?

We would take as models, in general, the University of Paris, the Universities of England before they were submerged in the Colleges, and the Universities of Germany.

In the creation of such a University we would at the very beginning collect a choice, varied, and ample library, second to none in the world in books to aid students in attaining ripe scholarship, and in promoting investigation in every department of knowledge—a library distinguished more for valuable and directly available resources of scholarship than for curious and antiquarian collections, estimated rather by the character than the number of its volumes. At the same time we would collect all the necessary apparatus for Physics and Chemistry; we would furnish a noble Observatory; we would found a rich Cabinet of Natural History; and we would open a gallery of the Fine Arts.

Thus with a full store of the material of science, literature, and the arts, would we lay the foundation of a University. We should thus meet aspirations and wants which, in our country, have hitherto been only disappointed, and call into the walks of learning, by commanding attractions, ingenuous minds that in despair have hitherto given themselves to other pursuits.

We would constitute four Faculties, a Faculty of Philosophy and Science, a Faculty of Letters and Arts, a Faculty of Law, and a Faculty of Medicine. Under these should be comprised a sufficient number of professorships to make a proper distribution of the various subjects comprehended under the general titles. These professorships should be endowed to an extent to afford the incumbents a competency independently of tuition fees. The necessity of such endowments must be obvious when we reflect that studious men require undisturbed minds, and that there are branches of knowledge which the interests of the world demand to have taught—such as Philology, Philosophy, the higher Astronomy, Mathematics, and Physics, while at the same time the number of students will be comparatively few.

It may be a question whether fees of tuition should be required of students, or whether the lectures, together with the libraries and cabinets, should be thrown open gratuitously to the public, as is done in the University of Paris. In this case the professorships, of course, would require to be more amply endowed.

The Professors of the different Faculties should be required to give courses of lectures, on the subjects assigned to them, to the Academical Members of the University. They should also be required to give popular courses to the public in general, on subjects selected by themselves.

By the *Academical* Members, we mean those who shall be admitted upon examination, or upon a Bachelor's degree from any College, and who shall enrol themselves as candidates for the University degrees.

These degrees may be of two grades. The lower grade may comprise Master of Arts, Doctor of Philoso phy, Doctor of Medicine, and Bachelor of Laws; the higher grade may comprise Doctor of Laws, Doctor of Theology, and other degrees to mark a high and honorable advance in Medicine, and in Philosophy, Science, Letters and Art.

Those of the first grade to be awarded after three or four years' study, and upon examination. Those of the second grade to be awarded as honorary degrees to men distinguished in the walks of life for their attainments and professional eminence, and to individuals who remain for a still longer term of years connected with the University in learned pursuits. It is, of course, understood that the provisions of the University are to be such as to enable students to pursue favorite branches of science, or learning in general, for an indefinite term of years.

One concurrent effect of this organization would be to elevate the character of Academical degrees, by making them the expression of real attainments, and honorable badges of real merit.

In connection with the popular courses of lectures, there should, also, be established courses particularly designed for the benefit of those engaged in commerce and the useful arts. This would give rise to another class of students besides the Academical, who might avail themselves of every advantage of the University possible to them under the degree of preparation they may have made, and under the pressure of daily business avocations. So also, others besides Academical students might attend the lectures in Law and Medicine, or indeed any courses which they might please to select, but without being considered as candidates for University degrees.

The result would be that the libraries, cabinets, laboratories, and lecture rooms of the University would become the resort of students of every grade; it would thus become the great centre of intellectual activity, and a fountain of learning open to the whole populace.

The different public libraries of the city might, also, be connected with it under their distinctive names; and new libraries might be founded by new donors, under new names, in the same connection, like the different libraries of the English Universities.

It will be remarked that we have omitted a Faculty of Theology in the constitution of this University. As each denomination of Christians has its peculiar Theological views and interests, it would be impossible to unite them harmoniously in one Faculty. It is most expedient, therefore, to leave this branch to the Theological Institutions already established by the several denominations. But still a connection of an unobjectionable character might be formed between Theological Institutions, especially those existing in this city, and the University, productive of very rich benefits. The students of the former might be admitted not only to the libraries of the latter, but also to the lectures on history, philosophy, philology, and general literature, when distinguished lecturers on these subjects gave promise of advantages additional to those enjoyed in the Theological Institutions. Indeed an arrangement might be made by which students undergoing prescribed examinations in philosophy, natural theology, philology, and history, and presenting certificates from their Professors of having completed satisfactorily their Theological courses, might be admitted to the degree of Bachelor in Theology. Students of the Free Academy, also, after having completed their courses in that Institution, might be admitted into the University as Academical Students, or otherwise according to the preparation they may have made.

Thus all our Institutions of learning would grow into a harmonious whole.

With respect to its religious and moral character it should embody in its constitution: First, an entire separation from ecclesiastical control and a renunciation of all sectarian partialities. Secondly, but as every thing that relates to human welfare, needs to be taken under the protecting and nurturing wings of Christianity, it should acknowledge Christianity to be the only true religion, the Bible to be of Divine inspiration, and the supreme rule of Faith and Duty, given freely to all men to be read and received with entire freedom of conscience and opinion.

To carry out these principles it should provide for an equal control of all denominations of Christians acknowledging these principles; it should institute a course of lectures on the evidences of Christianity and on Christian morality; and the reading of the Scriptures together with prayer should constitute a daily public service to be conducted by the Professors in the presence of the students.

No religious profession, however, should be required for admission to the University, but it should be open to students of all creeds as well as of all nations.

For the full development of such an Institution, ample funds are required; but that private munificence can accomplish it we fully believe. If the attention of our community can be aroused to the necessity, the interest, the glory of such a work, the accomplishment of it cannot be long delayed.

As examples of what private munificence can give, we need only appeal to various institutions of our land, and to the noble effort now making for Brown University. Nay, we need only look at the example of individuals in our own city with respect to the University of the City of New York; an institution which, although, like other similar institutions bearing the name of University, will claim to be only a College, and, therefore, not in its nature calculated to call forth as lively and as general an interest as the creation of a great University. There has been expended in money and liabilities on this institution, we have been informed, not less than four hundred thousand dollars, obtained chiefly by subscriptions.

Now all that will be required to put into full operation a University like the one we propose, will be about the sum expended on the above-named College. We will call the sum four hundred and fifty thousand dollars.

We can realize with this sum the following preparations and endowments:

A University building, for lecture-rooms, &c. -	$75,000
A Library building, - - - - -	50,000
Books—50,000 volumes,* - - -	50,000
Observatory, to be located on Staten Island, with Instruments, - - - -	20,000
Apparatus for Experiments in Physics and Chemistry,	4,000
Incipient Cabinet of Natural History, - -	5,000
Incipient Gallery of Fine Arts, - - -	6,000
Six fully endowed Professorships at $40,000 each, or ten partially endowed, at $24,000 each, -	240,000
Total, - -	$450,000 †

The rate of endowment for the professorships would be regulated, within certain limits, by the decision of the question, whether fees of tuition should be required of students, or not.

Such a foundation would ensure its permanent existence, and enable it to commence at once with all the forms of University education. This once accomplished, additions would afterwards be made as required, by a community now thoroughly awake to the interests of a great institution, and constantly experiencing its benefits.

Ten individuals giving 45,000 dollars each, would raise the sum required; or, fifty giving 9,000 dollars each; or, one hundred giving 4,500 dollars each; or,

* This is based on the average cost of the 20,000 volumes already collected in the Astor Library.

† If that noble public benefaction—The Astor Library, could become the centre of a University, and if the contemplated Observatory at Brooklyn could be connected with it, then $120,000 of the above estimate would be deducted.

one thousand giving 450 dollars each. Or, we might distribute it as follows:

Ten donors at	10,000	dollars	each,	$100.000
Twenty " "	5,000	"	"	100,000
Forty " "	2,500	"	"	100,000
Eighty " "	1,000	"	"	80,000
Five hundred	140	"	"	70,000
				$450,000

No one will doubt that our city contains the individuals who could do this with ease, by the above or by other distributions.

The men who should endow such an Institution, would raise to themselves a grander and more imperishable monument than the obelisks and pyramids of Egypt.

That the plan we have thus generally indicated is not chimerical is demonstrated by the fact that similar Institutions exist and flourish in France and Germany. Take the University of Berlin as an example, with its hundred professors and its two thousand students. These Universities are supported by the State. In Germany, several Universities receive from thirty to fifty thousand dollars annually. The University of Berlin must receive still more.

In our country we desire our Universities to be under the control neither of the Government, nor of any religious denomination, for we wish to preserve such Institutions free alike from political and sectarian influence and partialities. The different sects may have their Colleges and Theological Seminaries. But a great University should be the resort simply of scholars, and be scrupulously devoted to those general interests of learning which are common to men of every creed and of every political bias. Hence, it is required that they be established by private munificence, and be placed under a corporation of private individuals, comprising men devoted to science and letters and the commanding interests of education.

Did we live under a monarchical government, Universities might be established by the government, ana be connected with a national church; and then by taxation the people would be compelled to sustain them. Let it not be our reproach that monarchies alone can establish Universities: let us prove to the world that we can voluntarily create them, and that the spirit of a free people is mightier to the production of everything that can elevate and adorn humanity than the will of princes.

Universities are not the natural appendages or nurselings of monarchies. We have shown that they had their origin in the spirit of liberal and rational research, and that they were first established by individual enterprise. In Germany, particularly, so rife have been

liberal opinions, and so strong the advocacy of constitutional governments in the Universities, that they have at times called out the most vigorous persecution from the State.

They are eminently Institutions for the people, inasmuch as they place within the reach of all who are disposed to high education, all the means for its attainment. They are fountains whence universal knowledge may be diffused, and whose all-pervading influence goes to quicken, and to give order and consistency to every form of education.

That will be a proud day for the city of New York when it shall see such an Institution arise in the midst of its marts of business and its splendid palaces, and giving to its prosperity the crown of intellectual glory.

Why should we leave to another generation a work which we ourselves can accomplish, and which shall carry down our influence to the future under a form so good and beautiful, and so worthy of all that we claim for our enterprise, our far-seeing wisdom, our devotion to our country's welfare, and our confident hopes of its ultimate destiny?

Should we fail in our expectations of finding in the community men with views ready to grasp this design, and a liberality adequate to meet its demands, then why may not a band of assimilated scholars enter upon the work themselves, aided by a few liberal patrons of learning, or wholly unaided if need be, and renewing the scenes of past ages, institute courses of lectures like Roscelin, William of Champeaux, and Abelard?

Their success might at first be small ; b[illegible] their work ably, faithfully, and with indomit[illegible] verance, they would ultimately prevail, a[illegible] around them ingenuous young men, and awaken an enthusiasm for glorious scholarship, and so commend themselves and their work to the public, that wealth and influence would be enforced into their service by a charm which human nature has always obeyed. Universities meet a real want of humanity—a want which is now deeply felt in our own country ; and the existing Universities of the old world, which we now from a distance admire and long for, stand forth as guarantees of our success. We earnestly hope that the struggle of such an experiment, in our day, may not be called for ; but, if it is, are there not scholars who dare to make it?

APPENDIX.

I.

CATALOGUE OF LECTURES

Which were delivered in the University of Berlin during the winter term of 1829–30, *beginning with October* 29, *and continuing about six months.*

(The names of the Professors are given in order to show how many Lectures are delivered by the same Professors. The courses are substantially the same with those now delivered.)

THEOLOGY.

Theological encyclopædia and methodology (that is, general surve of theological science, and the proper method of studying it), by Prof. Hengstenberg, once a week. Historico-critical introduction to the Old Testament and the Apocrypha, by Lic. Uhlemann, four times a week. The exercises of an exegetical society on the passages of the prophets respecting the Messiah, are directed by the same professor, once a week, gratis. Genesis explained in Latin, four times a week, gratis. Principal parts of Genesis explained by Prof. Bellermann, twice a week. The Psalms explained, four times a week, by Dr. Benary. The Book of Job, Prof. Hengstenberg, four times a week. Biblical antiquities, by Lic. von Gerlach, four times a week. Introduction to the New Testament, by Lic. Rheinwald, four times a week. The Gospel of John, by Prof. Neander, five times a week. The First Epistle of Paul to the Corinthians, by Prof. Schleiermacher, four times a week. The Epistles to the Galatians, Ephesians, Philippians and

Colossians, by Lic. von Gerlach, four times a week. The two Epistles to the Corinthians, by Lic. Lommatyzsch, in Latin, five times a week. The Epistle of James, in Latin, the same, once a week, gratis. The exercises in disputation of the two exegetic societies are continued by the same, gratis. Epistles of John, by Lic. Rheinwald, twice a week, gratis. The life of Christ, by Prof. Schleiermacher, five times a week. Ecclesiastical history, from the time of Gregory VII., by Prof. Neander, five times a week. Introduction to scientific theology, both in a mo[illegible] doctrinal point of view, by Prof. Marheinecke, five times a w[illegible]iletics (all that relates to the preparation and delivery of [illegible]ourses), by Prof. Strauss, four times a week. Liturgics (th[illegible]edge of liturgies), by the same, gratis. Exercises in preaching, directed by the same, twice a week, gratis.

LAW.

General survey of legal science (*Juristische Encyclopædie*), by Prof. Biener and by Dr. Pütter, in Latin. Natural law, by Prof. Schmalz. Natural law, or philosophy of law, in connection with the general history of law, by Professor Gans, five times a week. Institutes of the Roman law, by Prof. Klenze, six times a week, and Prof. Gans, five times a week. Pandects, by Prof. Savigny. Law of inheritance, by Dr. Moosdorfer-Rossberger and by Dr. Radorff. External history of Roman law, by Dr. Moosdorfer-Rossberger, twice a week, gratis. History of the Roman civil process, by Dr. Pütter, two hours a week, in Latin. Ulpian's fragments explained by Dr. Radorff, twice a week, gratis. Canon law, by Prof. Schmalz, five times a week; by Dr. Laspeyres, five times a week; Dr. Moosdorfer-Rossberger, four times a week; Dr. Pütter at twelve o'clock, and Dr. Steltzer at three o'clock. History of the German empire and law by Professor Homeyer. History and antiquities of German law, with a short survey of the history of the empire, by Prof. Phillips. German private and feudal law, by Prof. von Lancizolle and by Prof. Phillips. Feudal law, by Dr. Moosdorfer-Rossberger, four times a week. Forest and game law, by Dr. Laspeyres. Criminal law, by Prof. Biener, with the criminal process, five times a week; Prof. Jarcke, the same, six times a week. History of criminal law, by Prof. Klenze, twice a week, gratis. On remarkable criminal cases, by Prof. Jarcke and Dr. Laspeyres. German territorial and federative law, by Prof. Schmalz, six times a week, gratis. Ancient constitution of the empire, and constitution of the confederacy, by Professor Lancizolle. On the constitution of Great Britain, by Professor Phillips, once a week. Common and Prussian civil process, by Professor Schmalz, four times a week; Professor Jarcke, five times a week; Dr. Moosdorfer-Rossberger, four times, and Dr. Radorff, four times a week. Practical exercises directed by Professor Schmalz, in connection with his lectures on the criminal process, on Saturdays. Dr. Moosdorfer-Rossberger offers to take charge of examinations and reviews of past studies.

MEDICINE.

Medical encyclopædia and methodology, by Prof. Casper, once a week, gratis. History of Medicine, by Prof. Hecker, twice a week, gratis. History of accouchement, by Dr. von Siebold, once a week. Lives and doings of great physicians, by Dr. Damerow, once a week, gratis. Explanations of the aphorisms of Hippocrates, continued by Prof. Bartels, once a week, gratis. Anatomy, six times a week, by Prof. Rudolphi. Complete anatomy, by Prof. Schlemm, four times a week. Osteology, by Prof. Knape, four times a week. Syndesmology, the same, twice a week, gratis. On aponeuroses, by Prof. S[illegible]m, twice a week, gratis. Splanchnology, by Prof. Knape, four [illegible]s a week. Anatomy of the organs of the senses and those of the fœtus, by Prof. Rudolphi, twice a week, gratis. Practical exercises in anatomy, directed by Profs. Knape and Rudolphi. Anthropology, by Prof. Kranichfeld, twice a week. Physiology, by Prof. Schultz, four times a week. Complete physiology, by Prof. Eck, six times a week. The first part of the theoretico-medical institutions, containing the elements of physiology, by the same, four times a week. Comparative physiology, by Prof. Horkel, six times a week. A survey of the history of life, the formation and propagation of organic bodies, by Dr. Brandt, once a week, gratis. Pathology, by Prof. Hufeland, junior, four times a week. General pathology, by Prof. Hecker, four times a week. Particular pathology, the same, six times a week. The same according to his own system, by Prof. Reich, six times a week. Pathological anatomy, by Prof. Rudolphi, four times a week. On regular and monstrous formations in natural bodies, by Dr. Ratzeburg, twice a week. Semeiotics, (the doctrine of symptoms), by Prof. Hufeland, junior, twice a week, gratis. Pharmacology, by Prof. Link, six times a week. The same, in connection with natural history and materia medica, explained by frequent demonstrations, with Dr. Ratzeburg and Dr. Brandt; the former teaches the mineralogical and zoological part, three times a week; the latter the botanical part, three times a week. Doctrine of physics, by Prof. Osann, six times a week. The same explained by exhibiting officinal plants and minerals, by Prof. Schultz, five times a week. Practical lectures on medicines, by Dr. Sundelin, four times a week. On officinal and poisonous plants, by Prof. Schultz, twice a week, gratis. On the mineral waters of Germany, by Prof. Osann, twice a week, gratis. The art of preparing recipes, treated generally and particularly, by Prof. Casper, twice a week; practical exercises continued. General therapeutics, by Dr. Oppert, three times a week. Dietetics and macrobiotics (q. v.), by Prof. Hufeland, senior, twice a week. Special pathology and therapeutics (q. v.), by Prof. Bartels, five times a week. The same, by Prof. Wagner, six times a week. Therapeutics of acute and chronic diseases in particular, by Prof. Horn, four times a week. Nosological therapeutics particularly treated, by Prof. Wolfart, four times a week. Second part of particular therapeutics, by Prof. Hufeland, junior, six times a week. On the diseases appearing during wars, in camps as well as in cities, by Prof. Wolfart, twice a week. The doctrine of mental disorders, with remarks, theoretical and practical, on their cure, by Dr. Damerow, four times a week. Doctrine of the diagnosis and cure of syphilitic diseases, by Prof. Horn, twice a week, gratis. The same, by Dr. Oppert, twice a week, gratis. Pathology and therapeutics of diseases having a material origin, by Dr. Sundelin, twice a week, gratis. Doctrine of the diseases of children, by Prof. Casper, twice a week, gratis. The same, by Prof. Reich, gratis. Doctrine of the diseases of children and women, by Dr. Friedländer, twice a week. Doctrine of the diseases of th[illegible]e, by Prof. Jüngken, five times a week, gratis. Instruction in op[illegible]ons of the eye, the same, *privatissime.** Anatomy, physiology, pathology and therapeutics of the human eye, in connection with the operations on it, by Prof. Kranichfeld, three times a week. General and special surgery, by Prof. Jüngken, six times a week. General surgery, by Prof. Kluge, twice a week. Akiurgy, or the doctrine of all surgical operations, by Prof. von Gräfe, four times a week. The same, by Prof. Rurt, six times a week. Operations on the dead subject are separate from these. On fractures and dislocations, by Prof. Kluge, once a week. Complete view of the means of curing diseases of the teeth, by Dr. Hesse, twice a week. All that relates to birth (*Geburtskunde*), by Prof. Busch, five times a week. Elements of midwifery, by Prof. Kluge, twice a week, gratis. The same; lectures on theoretical and practical obstetrics; and at two other hours exercises take place. Prof. Busch proposes to undertake a course of obstetrical operations, with exercises on the model. Prof. Busch will have, on Saturdays, an obstetrical examination. Theoretical and practical obstetrics, by Dr. Friedländer, three times a week. The same, by Dr. von Siebold, four times a week. He offers also to direct the exercises on the model. Clinical medical lectures in the Charité hospital, daily, by Prof. Bartels. Clinical exercises in the royal polyclinical institute, directed by Prof. Hufeland, senior, with Profs. Osann and Busse. Clinical directions for his hearers, by Prof. Wolfart. Directions for medical and forensic-medical practice, given by Prof. Wagner, six times a week. Clinical lectures on surgery, and diseases of the eye, in the royal clinico-surgical institute of the university, directed by Professor Gräfe, four times a week. Practical exercises at the sick-bed in surgical clinics, in the Charité hospital, directed by Prof. Rurt, four times a week. Polyclinics, by the same, every day. Practical exercises at the sick-bed of patients with disorders of the eye, in the Charité hospital, directed by Prof. Jüngken, five times a week. On venereal diseases, Prof. Kluge will give, twice a week, clinical instruction in the Charité hospital. Obstetrical clinics in the royal lying-in hospital,

* Lectures in the German universities are either *publice* (gratis), *privatim* (the general lectures, paid for by the student, from one louis d'or to five and six: these are meant if nothing is said in the catalogue), or *privatissime* (which are only for a few, who may choose to attend: at these, the price is higher, and the manner of instruction more familiar.)

and the polyclinics connected with it, directed four times a week, by Prof. Busch. Obstetrical clinics, by Dr. Friedlander, three times a week. Forensic anthropology, by Prof. Knape, three times a week. Forensic medicine for physicians and jurists, with practical exercises in the drawing up of opinions, &c., by Prof. Casper, three times a week. The same, by Dr. Barez, four times a week. Medical police, by Professor Wagner, twice a week, gratis. Dr. Sundelin offers to take charge of reviews of all parts of medical study. Veterinary art, by Dr. Recklebеn, three times a week. Doctrine of pestilential disorders among all domestic animals, in connection with forensic veterinary medicine, by the same, three times a week.

PHILOSOPHICAL SCIENCES.

Philosophical method, and the general survey of sciences, by Dr. Michelet, in connection with an introduction to the last systems of philosophy since Kant, four times a week, gratis. Foundation of philosophy, or the theory of all knowledge, by Dr. Schopenhauer, three times a week. Logic, five times a week, by Prof. Ritter. Logic, and a general survey of philosophy, by Dr. Beneke, four times a week. Logic and metaphysics, by Prof. Henning, five times a week. Ethics, by Prof. Ritter, four times a week. Psychology, and doctrine of mental diseases, by Dr. Beneke, five times a week. Psychology, six times a week, by Dr. von Keyserlingk. On the knowledge of God, by Prof. Ritter, once a week, gratis. Æsthetics, or general doctrine of arts, by Prof. Tölken, four times a week. Fundamental ideas of æsthetics, by Dr. Keyserlingk, four times a week. History of philosophy, by Prof. Hegel, five times a week. Critical history of distinguished metaphysical systems, by Dr. Beneke, once a week. Philosophy of history, by Prof. Stuhr, five times a week.

MATHEMATICAL SCIENCES.

Differential calculus, by Prof. Dirksen, three times a week. Analytical statics, the same, three times a week. Application of the integral calculus to geometry, by the same, once a week, gratis. Calculation of probabilities, by Dr. Dirichlet. Analysis of infinites, by the same. Introduction to algebra and analysis, once a week, gratis, by Prof. Ohm. Analytical plane and spherical trigonometry, also analytical geometry, four times a week, by the same. Differential and integral calculus, by the same, four times a week. Algebra, six times a week, by Prof. Ideler. On conic sections, three times a week, by the same. Planimetry, twice a week, by Prof. Grüson. Theoretical astronomy, three times a week, by Dr. Encke. Cosmography, twice a week, by Prof. Oltmanns.

NATURAL SCIENCES.

General physics, three times a week, by Prof. Erman. Magnetism and electricity, the same, three times a week. The first part of mechanical physics, four times a week, by Prof. Fischer. Experimental physics, four times a week, by Prof. Hermbstädt. The same, by Prof. Turte, twice a week. Elements of physics and chemistry, with experiments, by the same. General theoretical and practical chemistry, with experiments, six times a week, by Prof. Hermbstädt. Theoretical and practical pharmacy, or doctrine of the knowledge and preparation of chemical medicines, five times a week, by the same. Zoöchemy, once a week, by Prof. Mitscherlich, gratis. Experimental chemistry, four times a week, by the same. Theoretical chemistry, with particular reference to technology, five times a week, by Prof. Schubarth. Introduction to chemistry, by the same, once a week, gratis. Examinations in chemistry, by the same, three times a week. On chemical operations, once a week, by Prof. Hermbstädt. Pharmaceutic chemistry, three times a week, by Prof. Rose. On some organic officinal preparations, once a week, gratis, by the same. Exercises in chemical analysis, by the same, daily. General zoölogy, six times a week, by Prof. Lichtenstein. Natural history of the ruminant animals, by the same, twice a week, gratis. Natural history of the mammalia, by Dr. Wiegmann, twice a week, gratis. General zoölogy, five times a week, by the same. General entomology, twice a week, by Prof. Klug, gratis. On the laws of descriptive botany, once a week, gratis, by Prof. Hayne. Physiology of vegetables, especially of trees and shrubs, three times a week, by the same. On cryptogamic plants, gratis, by Prof. von Schlechtendal. On nutritive, officinal and poisonous plants, according to the natural families, four times a week, by the same. Mineralogy, six times a week, by Prof. Weiss. Descriptive crystallography, by the same, four times a week. The mineralogical part of the knowledge of soils for officers of the forest, twice a week, by the same.

POLITICAL AND ADMINISTRATIVE SCIENCES.

Public law and politics, by Prof. von Raumer, four times a week. On the modern public law and constitutions of government in both hemispheres, by Prof. Gans, once a week, gratis. *Cameral-Wissenchaft* (science of administration), four times a week, by Prof. Schmalz. History of the Prussian state since the beginning of the seventeenth century, with particular reference to the progress of public law, by Prof. von Henning, once a week, gratis. General statistics of Europe, four times a week, by Prof. Hoffmann. Statistics of the German confederation, twice a week, by Dr. Stein. Statistics of Prussia, twice a week, gratis, by Prof. Hoffmann. Public and adminstrative law of

Prussia, in connection with Prussian statistics, four times a week, by Prof. von Henning. Science of finances, or doctrine of the administration of public revenue, four times a week, by Prof. Hoffmann. Agricultural preparatory sciences, twice a week, by Prof. Störig. Science of agriculture, with particular reference to the wants of the *cameralist*, three times a week, by the same. On cattle, three times a week, by the same. General survey of forest sciences, four times a week, by Professor Pfeil. Knowledge and care of forests in a politico-economical respect, three times a week, by the same. Valuation and management of forests, three times a week, by the same. The same lecturer is ready to conduct an examination in all forest sciences, six times a week. *Cameral* chemistry, or application of chemistry to agriculture, the forest sciences, and the mechanic arts, with experiments, three times a week, by Prof. Hermbstädt.

HISTORY AND GEOGRAPHY.

History of antiquity, four times a week, by Dr. E. A. Schmidt. History of the middle ages, four times a week, by Prof. Wilken. Modern history, four times a week, by Prof. von Raumer. History of the eighteenth century, twice a week, gratis, by Dr. E. A. Schmidt. History of Prussia, from the beginning of the seventeenth century to the year 1813, six times a week, by Prof. Stuhr. History of the war of liberation, during 1813–15, twice a week, by the same. Historico-critical exercises are held once a week, by Prof. Wilken. General geography, five times a week, by Prof. Ritter. The same, by Prof. Zeune, twice a week. Hydrography and physiography of the West Indies and the neighboring coasts, once a week, by Prof. Oltmanns, gratis. Determination of geographical longitude and latitude from astronomical observations, twice a week, by the same.

HISTORY OF ART.

History, principles and monuments of Greek architecture, three times a week, by Prof. Tölken. History, principles and monuments of architecture in the middle ages, from the times of Justinian to the sixteenth century, by the same, twice a week. History of architecture among the Greeks, twice a week, gratis, by Prof. Hirt. Principles of the fine arts, by the same. On the art of painting among the ancients, gratis, once a week, by Prof. Tölken.

PHILOLOGICAL SCIENCES, &c.

General survey of the philological sciences and the method of studying them, four times a week, by Dr. Rötscher. General history of the literature of antiquity, the middle ages, and of modern times, five times a week, by Prof. Hotho. Greek antiquities, with particular reference to politics and the administration of justice, five times a week, by Prof. Böckh. Agamemnon and the Choephori of Æschylus, three times a week, by Prof. Lachmann. The Seven against Thebes of Æschylus, four times a week, by Dr. Lange. The Philoctetes and Antigone of Sophocles, in connection with an introduction, on the nature and history of the Greek tragedy, four times a week, by Dr. Heyse. The Clouds of Aristophanes, twice a week, by Dr. Rötscher, gratis. The Nicomachic ethics of Aristotle explained in connection with an introduction to the philosophy of Aristotle in general, twice a week, by Dr. Michelet. Thucydides, by Prof. Bekker, twice a week. Practical exercises in Latin and Greek, directed by the same. Latin style taught by Prof. Zumpt, four times a week. On Catullus, and the lyrical poetry of the Romans in general, with explanations of select poems of Catullus, twice a week, by Dr. Heyse. Cicero's fifth book against Verres, explained twice a week, gratis, by Prof. Zumpt. Histories of Tacitus, four times a week, by Böckh. Ancient geography of Palestine, once a week, gratis, by Prof. Ritter. Hebrew grammar, by Dr. Uhlemann, with a grammatical explanation of the book of Joshua, twice a week, gratis. Exegetical exercises in the Old Testament, directed by Dr. Benary, and difficult parts of the Hebrew grammar explained, three times a week, gratis. Chaldee grammar, with an explanation of select parts of the Chaldee Bible and Targums, by the same, three times a week, gratis. Elements of Syrian grammar, twice a week, by Prof. Hengstenberg. Arabian grammar, with explanation of the Arabian chrestomathy of Kosegarten, three times a week, by Prof. Wilken. Select Arabian historians and poets explained by Dr. Benary, four times a week. Grammar of Sanscrit, three times a week, gratis, by Professor Bopp. Select passages of the *Mahâ-Bhârata* explained by the same, twice a week, gratis. Persian grammar, by Wilken, once a week, gratis. Ancient German and Northern mythology, twice a week, gratis, by Prof. von der Hagen. On the ancient northern Edda-songs of the Nibelungs, the same, four times a week. History of the literature of the middle ages and modern times, four times a week, by the same. Elements of the old and middle High German grammar, five times a week, by Prof. Lachmann. Dante's Purgatory explained, twice a week, by Prof. F. W. V. Schmidt, gratis. History of modern poetry, four times a week, by the same. On the latest period of irony and mysticism in poetry and æsthetics, or on Frederic von Schlegel's *Novalis*, L. Tiek's and Solger's writings, once a week, by Prof. Hotho. Dante's *Divina Comedia* is explained in the Italian language, by Mr. Fabbrucci, gratis. Italian authors, such as his hearers may select, explained, by the same, four times a week. Elements of Italian grammar, *privatissime*, by the same. Shakspeare, by Dr. von Seymour. Private instruction in the English language, by the same. Some French tragedies explained, and the history of the French tragedy given in French, by Mr. Franceson. Instruction, *privatissime*, in French,

Spanish and Italian, by the same. The director Klein superintends the academical choir for church music, in which students can take part, gratis. Instruction in fencing and vaulting, by Mr. Felmy and Mr. Eiselen. The latter also gives instruction in gymnastics in general. Instruction in riding in the royal and several private riding schools.

PUBLIC LEARNED INSTITUTIONS.

The royal library is daily open for students. The observatory, the botanic garden, the anatomical, zootomical and zoological museum, the collection of minerals, of surgical instruments and bandages, of casts and works of art, &c., are used in the lectures, and can be visited by the students. Prof. Hengstenberg directs the exegetic exercises of the theological seminary; the exercises in ecclesiastical history and the history of dogmas are directed by Profs. Marheinecke and Neander. In the philological seminary, Prof. Böckh will hear the students explain Demosthenes, and direct the other exercises of the same. Prof. Lachmann will hear the students explain the odes of Horace.

[*Encylopædia Americana.*

II.

FACULTIES AND STUDENTS OF THE UNIVERSITY OF BERLIN, 1850.

	No. Professors.	No. Professors Extraordinary.	No. Lecturers, or Docentes.
THEOLOGY.	5	5	6
LAW.	9	4	5
MEDICINE.	12	7	18
PHILOSOPHY, COMPRISING METAPHYSICS, PHILOLOGY, HISTORY, ANTIQUITIES, MATHEMATICS, AND NATURAL SCIENCE.	36	28	30

BESIDES, FOUR MASTERS OF MODERN LANGUAGES.

MATRICULATED STUDENTS.

Theology,	184
Law,	570
Medicine,	223
Philosophy,	335
Total,	1312

STUDENTS WHO HEAR LECTURES, BUT ARE NOT MATRICULATED.

Surgery,	20
Pharmacy,	116
Students of the Frederick William Institute,	72
Students of the Medico-Chirurgical Academy, for the Army,	77
Students of the Architectural School,	229
Students of the Mining School,	21
Stipendiary Students of the Academy of Arts,	6
Students of the Horticultural Institute,	6
Total,	547
Whole No. Students,	1857

III.

FACULTIES OF THE UNIVERSITY OF LEIPSIC, 1850.

No. Professors.	No. Professors Extraordinary.	No. Docentes.
	THEOLOGY.	
6	6	2
	LAW.	
6	6	3
	MEDICINE.	
9	8	9
	PHILOSOPHY.	
21	7	7

IV.

Can the German Universities be accepted in full, as models for our own Universities?

As literal *Cyclopædias*, supplying all the means of the higher education—*l'instruction supérieure*—they undoubtedly can be thus accepted. In the details of the courses of lectures they cannot be thus accepted. The immense division of subjects which obtains in the German Universities may be questionable in itself, as begetting too great a comminution of ideas for a compact and orderly system. But granting that this objection is removed by the logical character of the division itself, and by the fact that the same professor lectures on several branches, so as to preserve a due relation of ideas to an organic whole in his particular department; still, the present condition of our learning, unused to the Germanic attenuation of thought, the difficulty, perhaps, at present of collecting a sufficient number of professors for so extensive a division of labor, and the impossibility of, at once, sustaining them, the obvious necessity of a somewhat gradual development of even the most perfect system, and the fact that our immediate wants can be fully met, and a powerful stimulus given to learning, and the first sure steps taken to reach the highest order of University education, with a more limited number of professorships embracing the cardinal branches of knowledge, and filled by men of undoubted qualifications, suggest an organization more circumscribed and compact than that of Germany, or that of France. It is mainly important that we begin on right principles and in a way to do an effective work, and leave the fecundity and ramifications of our growth to time and circumstances.

We would suggest, therefore, the following distribution of subjects in two of the faculties, leaving those of Law and Medicine to the determination of leading minds in their respective professions:—

FACULTY OF PHILOSOPHY AND SCIENCE.

1. Systematic Philosophy. 2. History of Philosophy. 3. The Philosophy of History. 4. Logic. 5. Ethics and the Evidences of Christianity. 6. The Higher Mathematics. 7. Astronomy. 8. Physics. 9. Chemistry. 10. Natural History.

FACULTY OF LETTERS AND ARTS.

1. Philology. 2. Greek Language and Literature. 3. Latin Language and Literature. 4. Oriental Languages. 5. Rhetoric and English Literature. 6. Modern Literature. 7. The History of the Fine Arts. 8. The Arts of Design.

These subjects might at first be distributed among ten or twelve Professors, aided by Lecturers, selected from among distinguished men, who, without formally accepting appointments in the University, might consent to deliver courses of Lectures during particular seasons of the year.

V.

PROGRAMME DES COURS

DE LA SORBONNE (FACULTÉS DES SCIENCES ET DES LETTRES);—DE LA FACULTÉ DE DROIT;—DE LA FACULTÉ DE MÉDECINE;—DE L'ÉCOLE DE PHARMACIE;—DU COLLÉGE DE FRANCE;—DE LA BIBLIOTHÈQUE NATIONALE;—DU MUSÉUM D'HISTOIRE NATURELLE

JOURS.	HEURES.	SECOND SEMESTRE 1850.	PROFESSEURS.
		SORBONNE (FACULTÉ DES SCIENCES).	
Lun.	8 h. 1/2..	Mécanique........................	Sturm.
	Midi 1/2.	Chimie...........................	Dumas *ou* Persoz.
	1 heure..	Astronomie mathématique...........	Cauchy.
	2 h. 1/2..	Mécanique physique et expérimentale..	Delaunay.
Mar.	10 h. 1/2.	Organographie végétale............	Aug. Saint-Hilaire.
	10 h. 1/2.	Calcul des probabilités............	Lamé.
	Midi 1/2.	Anatomie, Physiol. comp. et Zoologie....	De Blainville.
	2 h. 1/2..	Physique.........................	Pouillet.
Mer.	10 h. 1/2.	Botaniqué, Anat. et Physiol. végétales..	De Jussieu.
	10 h. 1/2.	Algèbre supérieure................	Duhamel.
	Midi 1/2.	Géométrie supérieure..............	Chasles.
	2 h. 1/2..	Géologie.........................	Constant-Prévost.
Jeu.	8 h. 1/2..	Calcul différentiel et intégral.........	Lefébure de Fourcy.
	Midi 1/2.	Chimie...........................	Dumas *ou* Persoz.
	1 heure..	Astronomie mathématique...........	Cauchy.
	2 h. 1/2..	Mécanique physique et expérimentale..	Delaunay.
Ven.	8 h. 1/2..	Mécanique........................	Sturm.
	10 h. 1/2.	Botanique., Anat. et Physiol. végétales..	De Jussieu.
	10 h. 1/2.	Algèbre supérieure................	Duhamel.
	Midi 1/2.	Géométrie supérieure..............	Chasles.
	2 h. 1/2..	Géologie.........................	Contrant-Prévost.
Sam.	8 h. 1/2..	Calcul différentiel intégral...........	Lefebure de Fourcy.
	10 h. 1/2.	Organographie végétale............	Aug. Saint-Hilaire.
	10 h. 1/2.	Calcul des probabilités............	Lamé.
	Midi 1/2.	Anat., Physiol. comp. et Zoologie......	De Blainville.
	2 h. 1/2..	Physique.........................	Pouillet.
		SORBONNE (FACULTÉ DES LETTRES).	
Lun.	9 heures.	Histoire de la Philosophie ancienne......	Jules Simon.
	10 h. 1/2.	Géographie.......................	Guigniaut.
	Midi	Philosophie.......................	E. Saisset.
	1 h. 1/2..	Littérature étrangère...............	Ozanam.
	3 heures.	Histoire de la Philosophie moderne......	Damiron.
Mar.	10 h. 1/2.	Poésie latine......................	Patin.
	Midi . . .	Histoire ancienne..................	Rosseeuw St-Hilaire.
	3 heures.	Histoire de la Philosophie moderne......	Damiron.

JOURS.	HEURES.	SECOND SEMESTRE 1850.	PROFESSEURS.
Mer.	9 heures.	Histoire moderne................	H. Wallon.
	10 h. 1/2.	Poésie latine..........................	Patin.
	Midi . . .	Poésie française..................	Caboche.
	1 h. 1/2..	Littérature grecque...............	Egger.
	3 heures.	Histoire de la Philosophie ancienne....	Jules Simon.
Jeu.	9 heures.	Philosophie.........................	A. Garnier.
	10 h. 1/2.	Géographie..........................	Guigniaut.
	Midi	Eloquence latine.....................	E. Havet.
	1 h. 1/2..	Littérature grecque.....................	Egger.
Ven.	10 h. 1/2.	Histoire moderne..................	H. Wallon
	Midi . . .	Eloquence latine..................	E. Havet.
	1 h. 1/2..	Philosophie........................	A. Garnier.
	3 heures.	Eloquence française..............	Géruzez.
Sam.	9 heures.	Eloquence française..............	Géruzez.
	10 h. 1/2.	Littérature grecque...............	Ch. Benoît.
	Midi . . .	Histoire ancienne.................	Rosseeuw St-Hilaire.
	1 h. 1/2..	Littérature étrangère.................	Ozanam.
	3 heures.	Poésie française........................	Caboche.

FACULTÉ DE DROIT.

JOURS.	HEURES.	COURS.	PROFESSEURS.
Lun., Mer., Ven.	8 heures.	Code civil français, 1re année...........	Valette.
	9 h. 3/4..	Id. id.	Bugnet.
	9 h. 1/2..	Code civil français, 2e année............	Duranton.
	11 h. 1/2.	Id. id.	Perreyve.
	8 heures.	Code civil français, 3e année.........	Demante.
	11 h. 1/2.	Id. id.	Oudot.
	1 heure..	Introduction générale à l'étude du droit	De Portets.
	1 heure..	Histoire du droit rom. et du droit franç..	Devalroger.
Mar., Jeu., Sam.	7 h. 1/2..	Droit crim. et législation pénale comp...	Ortolan.
	7 h. 1/2..	Droit administratif................	Roustain.
	8 heures.	Droit des gens...................	Royer-Collard.
	8 h. 3/4..	Procédure civile..................	Colmet Daage.
	9 heures.	Institutes de Justinien.............	Ducaurroy.
	10 h. 1/2.	Id. id.	Blondeau.
	9 heures.	Droit constitutionnel français.........	Vuatrin.
	10 heures	Pandectes.........................	Pellat.
	11 h. 1/4.	Code de Commerce...............	Bravard.
	11 h. 3/4.	Législation crim. et Procéd. civ. et crim.	Bonnier.

FACULTÉ DE MÉDECINE.

JOURS.	HEURES.	COURS.	PROFESSEURS.
L.,M.,V.	10 h. 1/2.	Histoire naturelle médicale..........	Richard.
	Midi	Accouch., malad. des fem. et des enf.....	Moreau.
	1 h. 1/2..	Physique médicale................	Gavarret.
	3 heures.	Pathologie médicale...............	Piorry.
Ma., Je., S.	10 h. 1/2.	Pharmacie et Chimie organique.........	Wurtz.
	3 heures.	Pathologie chirurgicale............	Richet.
	4 heures.	Anatomie pathologique............	Cruveilhier.
	1 heure..	Hygiène..............................	Royer-Collard.
	2 heures.	Thérapeutique et Matière médicale....	Trousseau

JOURS.	HEURES.	SECOND SEMESTRE 1850.	PROFESSEURS.
Tous les jours.	de 6 à 10 heures du matin.	Clinique chirurgicale............	Roux, à l'Hôtel-Dieu. Jarjavay, à l'hôp. de la F. Velpeau, à la Charité. Laugier, à la Pitié.
		Clinique médicale...............	Fouquier, à la Charité. Bouillaud, id. Chomel, à l'Hôtel-Dieu. Rostan, id.
		Clinique d'Accouchements.........	Dubois (Paul), à l'hôp. de [la F.

ÉCOLE DE PHARMACIE.

L. M. V.	Midi 1/2.	Manipulations....................	Gaultier de Claubry.
	3 heures.	Botanique. (Organog., Physiologie.)....	Chatin.
L. V.	8 heures.	Falsifications des médicaments........	Chevallier.
	10 heures	Hist. nat. des médicam. (Minéraux.)...	Guibourt.
Ma. Sa.	8 heures.	Pharmacie......................	Lecanu.
	9 h. 1/2..	Toxicologie.....................	Caventou.
	Midi...	Chimie organique................	Gaultier de Claubry.
J.		Botanique rurale. (Herborisations.)....	Chatin.

COLLÉGE DE FRANCE.

Lun.	10 h. 1/2.	Archéologie.....................	Lenormant.
	Midi...	Eloquence latine.................	Nisart.
	Midi...	Langue et littérature slave..........	Cyprien Robert.
	1 heure..	Histoire et morale................	Michelet.
	1 h. 1/2..	Langues hébraïq., chaldaïq. et syriaque.	Quatremère. [*ou* Franck
	1 h. 1/2..	Philosophie grecque et latine.........	Barthélemy St-Hilaire
	4 heures.	Langue et litt. chin. et tartare-mandchou.	Stanislas Julien.
Mar.	9 heures.	Droit de la nature et des gens.........	De Portets.
	10 h. 1/2.	Astronomie......................	Binet.
	11 heures	Histoire des législations comparées....	Laboulaye.
	11 h. 1/2.	Poésie latine....................	Tissot.
	Midi 1/2.	Chimie.........................	Pelouze.
	1 heure..	Langues et littér. de l'Europe méridion..	E. Quinet *ou* Dumesnil-
	1 heure..	Embryogénie comparée.............	Coste. [Michelet.
	1 heure..	Hist. naturelle des corps inorganiques...	Elie de Beaumont.
	1 h. 1/2..	Physique générale et mathématique....	Biot *ou* Bertrand.
	3 heures.	Langues et littér. d'origine germanique.	Philarète Chasles.
Mer.	8 h. 1/2..	Langue arabe....................	Caussin de Perceval.
	9 h. 1/2..	Langue et littérature sanskrite........	E. Burnouf.
	10 h. 1/2.	Langue persane..................	Jules Mohl.
	Midi...	Médecine.......................	Magendie *ou* Bernard.
	Midi...	Economie politique................	Michel Chevalier.
	Midi 1/2.	Langue turque...................	Alix Desgranges.
	Midi 1/2.	Physique générale et expérimentale....	Regnauld.
	Midi 1/2.	Langue et littérature grecque.........	Boissonade.
	1 h. 1/2..	Langues hébraïq., chaldaïq. et syriaque.	Quatremère.
	1 h. 1/2..	Histoire naturelle des corps organisés...	Duvernoy.
	3 h. 1/2..	Littérature française..............	J. J. Ampère.
Jeu.	8 heures.	Mathématiques...................	Hermite.
	10 h. 1/2.	Archéologie.....................	Lenormant.
	Midi 1/2.	Langue persane..................	Jules Mohl.
	1 heure..	Histoire et morale................	Michelet.
	4 heures.	Langue et litt. chin. et tartare-mandchou	Stanislas Julien.

JOURS.	HEURES.	SECOND SEMESTRE 1850.	PROFESSEURS.
Ven.	9 h. 1/2..	Langue arabe...........................	Caussin de Perceval.
	8 heures.	Langues et littér. de l'Europe méridion..	E. Quinet *ou* Dumesnil.
	9 h. 1/2..	Langue et littérature sanskrite.........	E. Burnouf. [Michelet.
	11 heures	Histoire des législations comparées.....	Laboulaye.
	Midi	Eloquence latine.......................	Nisart.
	Midi	Médecine................................	Magendie *ou* Bernard.
	Midi 1/2.	Langue turque...........................	Alix Desgranges.
	Midi 1/2.	Physique générale et expérimentale....	Regnault.
	Midi 1/2.	Langue et littérature grecque..........	Boissonade.
	1 h. 1/2..	Philosophie grecque et latine...........	Barthélemy St-Hilaire
	1 h. 1/2..	Histoire naturelle des corps organisés..	Duvernoy. [*ou* Franck.
	2 heures.	Physique générale et mathématique.....	Biot *ou* Bertrand.
Sam.	8 heures.	Mathématiques...........................	Hermite.
	9 heures.	Droit de la nature et des gens...........	De Portets.
	9 heures.	Langue et littérature slave............	Cyprien Robert.
	10 h. 1/2.	Langues et littér. d'origine germanique..	Philarète Chasles.
	10 h. 1/2.	Astronomie..............................	Binet.
	11 h. 1/2.	Poésie latine............................	Tissot.
	Midi	Economie politique......................	Michel Chevalier.
	Midi 1/2.	Chimie..................................	Pelouze.
	1 heure..	Embryogénie comparée..................	Coste.
	1 heure..	Hist naturelle des corps inorganiques..	Elie de Beaumont,
	3 h. 1/2..	Littérature française....................	J.-J. Ampère.

BIBLIOTHÈQUE NATIONALE (rue Neuve-des-Petits-Champs, 12).

L. M. V.	9 h. 1/2..	Cours de chinois moderne...............	Bazin.
	11 heures	Cours d'arabe vulgaire...................	Caussin de Perceval.
	2 h. 1/2..	Cours de malay et de javanais..........	Ed. Dulaurier.
	4 heures	Cours d'arménien.........................	Le Vaillant de Florival
L. V.	7 h. du s.	Cours de persan..........................	Quatremère.
M. J. S.	9 h. 3/4..	Cours d'hindoustani......................	Garcin de Tassy.
	2 h. 1/2..	Cours d'arabe............................	Reinaud.
	4 heures.	Cours de turc............................	Louis Dubeux.
M. S.	11 heures	Cours de grec et de paléographie grecque	Hase.

MUSÉUM D'HISTOIRE NATURELLE (Jardin des Plantes).

L. M. V.	10 heures	Minéralogie..............................	Dufrénoy.
	Midi	Botanique et Physique végétale.........	Ad. Brongniart.
M.. J.. S.	10 h. 1/4.	Chimie appliquée.........................	Chevreul.
	1 heure..	Physiologie comparée...................	Flourens.
	3 heures.	Hist. nat. des Crustacés, des Arachnides et des Insectes	Milne Edwards.
M. S.	10 heures	Culture..................................	Decaisne.
D.		Botanique dans la campagne............	De Jussieu.

The University of Paris is the ancient University, founded by William of Champeaux, in 1109. The *Sorbonne* is the title given to one of the Colleges founded by Robert de Sorbonne, an ecclesiastic of the thirteenth century. It was strictly a school of Theology ; and, although only one of the four constituent parts of the Faculty of Theology in the University of Paris, it attained such eminence that it frequently gave its name to the whole faculty ; and even graduates of the University, not belonging to this College, were wont to style themselves doctors, or bachelors of the Sorbonne. The Sorbonne, on account of its reputation, was appealed to to decide questions in Theology and Morals.

The buildings of the College are now occupied by the three faculties of Theology, Science, and Literature of the Académie Universitaire of Paris.

The *Collége Royal de France* was instituted by Francis I., in 1530. He created twelve chairs for instruction in Greek, Hebrew, Eloquence, Philosophy, and Medicine. Since then various additions have been made, until now the number of chairs amounts to twenty-four. The courses are gratuitous. The Oriental Languages hold a very conspicuous place.

The University of France is the work of Napoleon. " Ce grand esprit reconnut tout d'abord que l'éducation publique devait être la base de l'ordre nouveau. Nulle matière ne l'occupa davantage. Il consulta les hommes les plus différentes ; il eut sous les yeux les projets les plus divers. Il répetait sans cesse cette phrase celebre de Leibnitz : Donnez-moi l'instruction publique pendant un Siecle, et je changerai le monde."*

* Cousin.

He instituted a great system of national education comprising three degrees, *l'instruction primaire, l'instruction secondaire, l'instruction supérieure.* The University comprehends the last two. To the *instruction secondaire* belong the Colleges. Of these about three hundred and twenty are *Collèges communaux* scattered through the large towns. They are supported by the towns, the heads and professors being paid out of the revenues of the Communes. Forty of them are royal Colleges, *les lycées ou Collèges royaux.* The directors and professors in these are paid by the State. The *Collège royal de France* is one of these.

To the *instruction supérieur* belong the faculties of the University proper: the faculties of Theology, Law, Medicine, Science, and Letters.

The Institute National de France is a society of learned men, instituted not for the purpose of giving instruction, but for the purpose of advancing science and the arts by original and uninterrupted researches, by the publication of discoveries, and by correspondence with learned societies, and learned men in other countries. It consists of resident members, and corresponding members native and foreign, and associate foreign members. Of the first there are nearly two hundred, of the last two, more than two hundred. The resident members and the five perpetual secretaries receive salaries.*

The Institute is distributed into five Academies—The Academy of the French language and literature, The Academy of Inscriptions and Belles-Lettres, The Academy of the Fine Arts, The Academy of Sciences, and The Academy of Moral and Political Sciences.

* The resident members receive each 1500 francs, the secretaries 6000 francs, per annum.

www.ingramcontent.com/pod-product-compliance
Lightning Source LLC
LaVergne TN
LVHW021424110826
845150LV00007B/2076

* 9 7 8 1 4 2 5 5 0 8 1 1 1 *